THE
EXTRAVAGANT
Love
OF JESUS

The Extravagant Love of Jesus

Jesus

He was born some two thousand
years ago and yet still lives.
He gave us everything and yet still gives.
He gives us life eternally and died on the old-rugged cross;
On top of Mount Calvary so all souls wouldn't be lost.
If you're still suspicious,
He walked upon the sea, He healed a man born blind,
Preached in Galilee, and died for all mankind.
Now do you know His name?
Yes, His name is Jesus, and His love is our gain.

~Melvin Musgrove

THE
EXTRAVAGANT
Love
OF JESUS

Table of Contents

JESUS' EXTRAVAGANT *Love* SAVES

For God so loved the world,
that he gave his only begotten Son,
that whosoever believeth in him
should not perish,
but have everlasting life.

JOHN 3:16 KJV

JESUS REALLY DOES LOVE YOU

E very Sunday afternoon, after the morning service at their church, the Pastor and his 11-year-old son would go out into their town and hand out Gospel tracts. This particular Sunday afternoon, as it came time for the Pastor and his son to go to the streets with their tracts, it was very cold outside as well as pouring down rain. The boy bundled up in his warmest and driest clothes and said "Okay Dad, I'm ready."

His Pastor Dad asked, "Ready for what?"

"Dad, it's time we gather our tracts together and go out."

Dad responds, "Son, it's very cold outside and it's pouring down rain."

The boy gives his Dad a surprised look, asking, "But Dad, aren't people still going to Hell, even though it's raining?"

Dad answers, "Son, I am not going out in this weather." Despondently the boy asks, "Dad, can I go—Please?"

His father hesitated for a moment then said, "Son, you can go. Here are the tracts; be careful son."

"Thanks, Dad!" And with that he was off and out into the rain. This 11-year-old boy walked the streets of the town going door-to-door and handing everybody he met in the street a Gospel tract.

After 2 hours of walking in the rain he was soaking bone-chilled wet and down to his very last tract. He stopped on a corner and looked for someone to hand a tract to but the streets were totally deserted. Then he turned toward the first home he saw and started up the sidewalk to the front door and rang the doorbell. He rang the bell—but nobody answered. He rang it again and again but still no one answered. He waited but still no answer. Finally, this 11-year-old trooper turned to leave but something stopped him. Again, he turned to the door and rang the bell and knocked loudly on the door with his fist. He waited, something holding him there on the front porch. He rang again, and this time the door slowly opened.

Standing in the doorway was a very sad looking elderly lady. She softly asked, "What can I do for you, son?"

With radiant eyes and a smile that lit up her world, this little boy said, "Ma'am, I'm sorry if I disturbed you, but I just want to tell you that Jesus Really Does Love You! I came to give you my very last Gospel tract, which will tell you all about Jesus and His great love."

With that, he handed her his last tract, and turned to leave.

She called to him as he departed, "Thank you, son! And God bless you!"

Well, the following Sunday morning in church, Pastor Dad was in the pulpit and as the service began he asked, "Does anybody have a testimony or want to say anything?"

Slowly, in the back row of the church, an elderly lady stood to her feet. As she began to speak, a look of glorious radiance came from her face. "None of you in this church know me. I've never been here before. You see, before last Sunday I was not a Christian. My husband has passed on, some time ago, leaving me totally alone in this world. Last Sunday, being a particularly cold and rainy day, it was even more so in my heart . . . as I came to the end of the line where I no longer had any hope or will to live. So I took a rope and a chair and ascended the stairway into the attic of my home. I fastened the rope securely to a rafter in the roof then stood on the chair and fastened the other end of the rope around my neck. Standing on that chair, so lonely and brokenhearted, I was about to leap off when suddenly the loud ringing of my doorbell downstairs startled me. I thought, 'I'll wait a minute, and whoever it is will go away.' I waited and waited—but the ringing doorbell seemed to get louder and more insistent and then the person ringing also started knocking loudly. I thought to myself again, 'Who on earth could this be? Nobody ever rings my bell or comes to see me!' I loosened the rope from my neck and started for the front door, all the while the bell rang louder and louder. When I opened the door and looked I could hardly believe my eyes! There on my front porch was the most radiant and angelic little boy I had ever seen in my life! His smile! Oh, I could never describe it to you! And the words that came from his mouth caused my heart, that had long been dead, to leap to life as he exclaimed with a cherub-like voice, 'Ma'am, I just came to tell you that JESUS REALLY DOES LOVE YOU.' Then he gave me this Gospel tract that I now hold in my hand. As the little angel disappeared back out into the cold and rain, I closed my door and read slowly every word of this Gospel tract. Then I went up to my attic to get my rope and chair. I wouldn't need them any more. You see, I am now a happy child of the King, and since the address of your church was on the back of this Gospel tract I have come here to personally say, 'Thank you to God's little angel who came just in the nick of time, and by so doing, spared my soul from an eternity in Hell.'"

There were now no dry eyes in the church. As shouts of praise and honor to the Lord resounded off the very rafters of the building, Pastor Dad descended from the pulpit to the front pew where the little angel was seated. He took him in his arms and sobbed uncontrollably. The answer to true peace and happiness can only be found in Jesus...all because of His love, His extravagant love.

—Author Unknown

Let your light so shine before men, that they may see
your good works and glorify your Father in heaven.

MATTHEW 5:16 NKJV

❖

"Come now, let us argue this out," says the Lord.
"No matter how deep the stain of your sins, I can remove it.
I can make you as clean as freshly fallen snow.
Even if you are stained as red as crimson,
I can make you as white as wool."

ISAIAH 1:18 NLT

❖

O, THE BLOOD OF JESUS;

O, THE BLOOD OF JESUS;

O, THE BLOOD OF JESUS;

IT WASHES WHITE AS SNOW!

~ ANON

❖

But if we are living in the light of God's presence,
just as Christ is, then we have fellowship with each other,
and the blood of Jesus, his Son, cleanses us from every sin.

I JOHN 1:7 NLT

JESUS'
EXTRAVAGANT *Love*
IS
AVAILABLE

Draw near to God and
He will draw near to you.

JAMES 4:8 NASB

JESUS CAME OUT OF LOVE

The play was about to begin, but her daddy was not sitting in the audience with the family waiting to see her performance. One of three surgeons in a small town meant that his schedule did not belong to him. He was often on-call, even when he wasn't on-call. Much to the chagrin of his daughter, a car accident involving serious injuries required all three doctors be in surgery that night. She had long ago accepted the fact that her dad might miss some of her activities, but this one was so special to her and she found the disappointment almost too much to bear.

Struggling to hold back the tears as the play she had practiced for the past six weeks was about to begin required all the strength she could muster. She so wanted to have a positive attitude, but her heart was too heavy and the emotion was evident. She knew her mother, brother and sister, and her grandparents on both sides were anxiously looking forward to her part. She had the starring role. As the music crescendo intensified she began to move on stage as tears fell down her cheeks. As she looked out at the audience she saw a lone man standing next to the double doors in the back of the auditorium. It was her daddy. After the play, she met up with her family, her daddy was not there. Sharing her joy with her mother over seeing her daddy at her play, was followed by a question ...

"How? How did he come?" Her mother answered, "He came out of love." Jesus came out of Love for us. He came just like the loving daddy, who made a way, so he could be there for his child. Jesus made a way for us, His children. He is always watching our life...He is always available. What extravagant love! —PMH

❖

For today in the city of David
there has been born for you a
Savior, who is Christ the Lord.

LUKE 2:11 NASB

❖

I am the light of the world; he
who follows Me shall not walk in the
darkness, but shall have the light of life.

JOHN 8:12 NASB

'THE BLESSING FROM THE CLOUD THAT SHOWERS,

IN WONDROUS TWOFOLD BIRTH

OF HEAVEN IS, AND EARTH

HE IS BOTH YOURS, YE HOSTS, AND OURS:

HOSANNAH,

DAVID'S SON,

FOR VICTORY IS WON!

HE LEFT US WITH A BLESSING HERE,

AND TOOK IT TO THE SKY;

THE BLESSING FROM ON HIGH

BESPEAKS TO US HIS PRESENCE NEAR:

HOSANNAH,

DAVID'S SON,

FOR VICTORY IS WON!'

~ FROM AN ASCENSION HYMN

If you continue in My word,
then you are truly disciples of Mine;
and you will know the truth,
and the truth will make you free.

JOHN 8:31, 32 NASB

✝ Sweet Jesus, You came to earth
in simple splendor to show us Your
great love in life, and in death.
How grateful we are that You came.
Humble us, we pray, as we seek
to learn of You and as we learn and
receive that greatest love we can ever
know...the love of Jesus. *Amen*

JESUS' EXTRAVAGANT *Love* IS ABUNDANT

And God is able to make all grace
abound to you, that always having
all sufficiency in everything, you
may have an abundance
for every good deed.

II CORINTHIANS 9:8 NASB

HERS, TOO, WAS ABUNDANT LOVE

B eing raised very poor, she had learned early in life that everything she owned came with a great price. Once married, and with seven children to care for, it was important that she help her children to recognize the value of the things they had. She wanted them to appreciate and care for their belongings, whether a hand-me-down or something new. Every gift was to be treasured because she knew that every gift came from a loving Father. He met her needs and she knew He would always do so.

She had a good job before she married and was able to purchase a lovely green cashmere store-bought coat. It was the first store-bought coat she had ever owned and it was beautiful on her, with her lovely deep auburn hair. She took great pains to make certain the coat was neatly put away after church each Sunday. She covered it with a sheet to keep any dust from collecting on it and she brushed it before and after each time she wore it. Never in her life had she been able to walk into a store and purchase a new coat for herself. It was special.

One year, the pot belly stove in the kitchen and the fireplace in the living room were no match for the bitterly cold winter wind that easily made its way through the large cracks in the un-insulated walls of the little four room house she and her family lived in. Her mother's heart could not stand the thought of her children not being warm. As she gingerly made her way around the bedroom checking each of them, two girls in one bed, two girls in another, her two sons on the bunk beds, and the baby in the crib, she realized there was not enough cover to keep all of them warm. She tucked each of her little ones in as best she could then went to stoke the fires. Not satisfied, she returned to check on her children one more time. Two of them were cold and she had to make certain they were protected from the artic air that was sweeping deep down into the South on that particular night. There was no decision to be made...no other options available to her. She went to the tiny closet, removed the sheet from her beautiful green cashmere store-bought coat, took it to the bed of her two daughters that needed more cover for the night and gently wrapped them in its warmth. Satisfied, she went to bed.

I often wondered what she was thinking when she went back to bed that night. Yes, I was there...wrapped up warmly in my mother's beautiful green cashmere store-bought coat. The coat that looked so good on her with her beautiful deep dark auburn hair. That was many years ago, and I saw my mother make hundreds of sacrifices for her children during the next thirty years. She was one of the

most giving people I ever knew. She had an abundance of love to
share with so many. She went home to heaven last year. After she
passed away, several of her things were divided among the family
and one of the things that came to me was her last green store-
bought coat, a lovely green store-bought coat that I will wear in her
memory. Each time I wear it, I am reminded that she loved her first
lovely green cashmere store-bought coat, but she had her priorities
in the right place, and she loved her children more. The greatest
expression of love ever is the gift of Jesus who gave His life so we
can be wrapped in the warmth of His love. His love is abundant and
forever. —PMH

*Every good thing given and every
perfect gift is from above, coming
down from the Father of lights,
with whom there is no variation
or shifting shadow.*

JAMES 1:17 NASB

JESUS—THE NAME THAT CHARMS OUR FEARS,

THAT BIDS OUR SORROWS CEASE;

'TIS MUSIC IN THE SINNER'S EARS,

'TIS LIFE, AND HEALTH, AND PEACE.

~CHARLES WESLEY

❖

*T*hank You, Precious Jesus, for the abundant love that is available to Your children every moment of every day. How blessed we are to know You and Your abundant love. *Amen*

❖

But God, being rich in mercy, because
of His great love with which He loved us,
even when we were dead in our transgressions,
made us alive together with Christ,
by grace you have been saved...

EPHESIANS 2:4, 5 NASB

LOVE LIFTED ME

I was sinking deep in sin, far from the peaceful shore.

Very deeply stained within, sinking to rise no more;

But the Master of the sea heard my despairing cry,

From the waters lifted me, now safe am I.

Love lifted me! Love lifted me!

When nothing else could help, Love lifted me!

All my heart to Him I'll give, ever to Him I'll cling,

In His blessed presence live, ever His praises sing.

Love so mighty and so true merits my soul's best songs;

Faithful, loving service, too, to Him belongs.

Love lifted me! Love lifted me!

When nothing else could help, Love lifted me!

Souls in danger, look above, Jesus completely saves;

He will lift you by His love, out of the angry waves.

He's the Master of the sea, billows His will obey;

He your Saviour wants to be—

BE SAVED TODAY!

Love lifted me! Love lifted me!

When nothing else could help,

Love lifted me!

– JAMES ROWE

JESUS' EXTRAVAGANT *Love* IS INTIMATE

I am the good shepherd; and I know
My own, and My own know Me ...

JOHN 10:14 NASB

HE'S COUNTING

"How many chemo treatments will I have before my hair starts to fall out?" I asked my long-time friend, who had recently become my oncologist. He looked at me with a gentle, but serious and confident smile. "Probably after the first one," he said. "Really," I gulped. I didn't realize it could happen so soon. My diagnosis of breast cancer had been a complete surprise to me. I had zero symptoms, not even a lump. But a routine yearly mammogram revealed "areas of concern," and a subsequent needle biopsy confirmed that I had cancer. Even though I was told that we had caught it in the early stages, the removal of both my breasts, and twenty-one lymph nodes plus complete body scans revealed that the cancer had spread not only to my lymph nodes, but there were four spots on my liver. This hurled me into stage four cancer. I learned with this new educational experience that there are only four stages. So early stages or not, this was a very aggressive cancer. That is why I sat in the oncologist's office asking about my hair loss that would happen sooner than I had expected. I had to wait a few weeks before that first chemo treatment to allow my body to regain strength from the mastectomy. I was glad to have time to cry out to the Lord Jesus, and lean hard on Him. I had known him as my personal Savior since I was seven years old. "Lord, are you sure this is supposed to happen to me?" After all, I had led a very blessed life. My husband of thirty-five years loved the Lord and me. We had served Him together for many years. Our two children were walking with the Lord, and were establishing Christian homes of their own. "Why me and why now?" I questioned. But the longer I stayed in the Lord's presence, the more I understood, "Why not me, and why not now?" After all, does the Lord Jesus just love me when things are going the way I think they should? I knew the answer to that. The Lord loves me with an everlasting love to the smallest details of my being. While I was still basking in His presence, He reminded me that, "the very hairs of your head are all numbered." (Matthew 10:30) Jesus said that. How did He know? That truth had not been taught in the Old Testament. Jesus said it when He was walking on this earth. He said it because He knows it is true, because He is God, and because He does the counting. My husband and my children love me but they don't keep count of the very hairs of my head, but Jesus does. Now that is "extravagant" love. To love to that detail is going to the extreme. But I know His love for me goes to the extreme. He proved it on Calvary, and in the counting of the hairs of my head. So...when the first few hairs remained on my pillow the night after my first chemo treatment, it was O.K. because the One who loves me to the smallest details of my being was counting. —Teresa King

The very hairs of your head are all numbered.

MATTHEW 10:30 NKJV

◆

JESUS ALWAYS ANSWERS IN THE DEEPS,

NEVER IN THE SHALLOWS OF OUR SOUL.

~ ANON

◆

TRUE LOVE DOESN'T HAVE A HAPPY ENDING:

TRUE LOVE DOESN'T HAVE AN ENDING.

~ ANON

◆

THERE IS NO GREATER INVITATION

TO LOVE THAN LOVING FIRST.

~ ST. AUGUSTINE

WHERE THERE IS GREAT LOVE,

THERE ARE ALWAYS MIRACLES.

~ W. CATHRE

❖

ARE WE WEAK AND HEAVY-LADEN,

CUMBERED WITH A LOAD OF CARE?

PRECIOUS SAVIOUR, STILL OUR REFUGE;

TAKE IT TO THE LORD IN PRAYER.

~JOSEPH SCRIVEN

❖

LOVE ME WHEN I LEAST DESERVE IT,

BECAUSE THAT'S WHEN I REALLY NEED IT.

~ SWEDISH PROVERB

JESUS' EXTRAVAGANT *Love* IS VICTORIOUS

... thanks be to God, who gives us the victory through our Lord Jesus Christ.

I CORINTHIANS 15:57 NASB

JESUS IN THE HOUSE

One day he decided to invite the Lord to come home and stay with him. When the Lord arrived, this young man offered him the very best room in the house. The room was upstairs and at the end of the hall. "This room is yours, Jesus! Stay as long as you like and you can do whatever you want to in this room, remember Jesus, it's all yours."

That evening after he had retired for the night there came a loud knocking at the front door. The young man pulled on his robe and made his way downstairs. When he opened the door he found that the devil had sent three of his demons to attack him. He quickly tried to close the door but one of the demons kept sticking his foot in.

Sometime later, after a great struggle, he managed to slam the door shut and returned to his room totally exhausted. "Can you believe that," the man thought. Jesus is upstairs in my very best room sleeping while I am down here battling demons. Oh, well, maybe he just didn't hear. He slept fitfully that night.

The next day things went along as normal and, being tired as he was, the young man retired early that evening. Along about midnight, there came such a terrible ruckus at the front door that the young man was sure that whatever it was would tear the door down. He stumbled down the stairs once again and opened the door to find that were dozens of demons now trying to get into his beautiful home. For more than three hours he fought and struggled against the demons from hell, and finally overtook them enough to shut the door against their attack. All energy seemed to fail him. He really didn't understand this at all. 'Why won't the Lord come to my rescue? Why does he allow me to fight all by myself? I feel so alone.' Troubled, he found his way to the sofa and fell into a restless sleep.

The next morning he decided to inquire of the Lord about the happenings of the last two evenings. Quietly he made his way to the elegant bedroom where he had left Jesus. "Jesus," he called as he tapped at the door. "Lord, I don't understand what is happening. For the last two nights I have had to fight the demons away from my door while you laid up here sleeping. Don't you care about me? Did I not give you the very best room in the house?" He continued on, "I just don't understand, I really thought that once I invited you in to live with me that you would take care of me and I gave you the best room in my house and everything. What more can I do?"

"My precious child," Jesus spoke so softly. "I do love and care for you. I protect all that you have released into my care. But, when you invited me to come here and stay, you brought me to this lovely room and you shut the door to the rest of your house. I am Lord of this room but I am not Master of this house. I have protected this room and no demon may enter here."

"Oh, Lord, please forgive me. Take all of my house—it is yours. I am so sorry that I never offered you all to begin with. I want you to have control of everything." With this he flung open the bedroom door and knelt at Jesus' feet. "Please forgive me Lord for being so selfish." Jesus smiled and told him that He had already forgiven him and that He would take care of things from now on.

That night as the young man prepared for bed he thought, 'I wonder if those demons will return, I am so tired of fighting them each and every night.' But, he knew that Jesus said that he would take care of things from now on.

Along about midnight the banging on the door was frightening. The young man slipped out of his room in time to see Jesus going down the stairs. He watched in awe as Jesus swung open the door, no need to be afraid. Satan stood at the door, this time demanding to be let in. "What do you want, Satan?" the Lord asked.

The devil bowed low in the presence of the Lord, "So sorry, I seem to have gotten the wrong address." And with that, he and the demons all ran away. There is a moral to this tale. Jesus wants all of you, not just a part. He will take all that you give Him, but nothing more. How much of your heart have you given to Jesus? Are you keeping a portion of it away from Him? Perhaps the attacks are coming more and more each day. Why not let the Lord fight the battles for you? He is always victorious! —Author Unknown

JESUS LOVES ME

Jesus loves me this I know, for the Bible tells me so.
Little ones to Him belong, they are weak, but He is strong.
Yes, Jesus loves me. Yes, Jesus loves me.
Yes, Jesus loves me, the Bible tells me so.
Jesus loves me! He who died, heaven's gates to open wide;
He will wash away my sin. Let His little child come in.
Yes, Jesus loves me. Yes, Jesus loves me.
Yes, Jesus loves me, the Bible tells me so.
Jesus loves me! He will stay close beside me all the way;
If I love Him, when I die He will take me home on high.
Yes, Jesus loves me, Yes, Jesus loves me.
Yes, Jesus loves me, the Bible tells me so.

–ANNA BARTLETT WARNER

'TIS SO SWEET TO TRUST IN JESUS

'Tis so sweet to trust in Jesus,
And to take Him at His word;
Just to rest upon His promise,
And to know, "Thus saith the Lord."
O how sweet to trust in Jesus,
Just to trust His cleansing blood;
And in simple faith to plunge me
'Neath the healing, cleansing flood!
Yes, 'tis sweet to trust in Jesus,
Just from sin and self to cease;
Just from Jesus simply taking
Life and rest, and joy and peace.
I'm so glad I learned to trust Thee,
Precious Jesus, Savior, friend;
And I know that Thou art with me,
Wilt be with me to the end.
Jesus, Jesus, how I trust him!
How I've proved Him o'er and o'er!
Jesus, Jesus, precious Jesus,
O for grace to trust Him more!

~LOUISA M. R. STEAD

JESUS' EXTRAVAGANT *Love* REACHES OUT

It is more blessed to give than to receive.

ACTS 20:35 NASB

LOVE AND RECOGNITION

A teacher in New York decided to honor each of her seniors in high school by telling them the difference they each made. Using a process developed by H. Bridges of California, she called each student to the front of the class, one at a time. First she told them how the student made a difference to her and the class. Then she presented each of them with a blue ribbon imprinted with gold letters which read, "Who I Am Makes a Difference." Afterwards the teacher decided to do a class project to see what kind of impact recognition would have on a community. She gave each of the students three more ribbons and instructed them to go out and spread this acknowledgment ceremony. Then they were to follow up on the results, see who honored whom and report back to the class in about a week.

One of the boys in the class went to a junior executive in a nearby company and honored him for helping him with his career planning. He gave him a blue ribbon and put it on his shirt. Then he gave him two extra ribbons, and said, "We're doing a class project on recognition, and we'd like you to go out, find somebody to honor, give them a blue ribbon, then give them the extra blue ribbon so they can acknowledge a third person to keep this acknowledgment ceremony going. Then please report back to me and tell me what happened."

Later that day the junior executive went in to see his boss, who had been noted, by the way, as being kind of a grouchy fellow. He sat his boss down and he told him that he deeply admired him for being a creative genius. The boss seemed very surprised. The junior executive asked him if he would accept the gift of the blue ribbon and would he give him permission to put it on him. His surprised boss said, "Well, sure."

The junior executive took the blue ribbon and placed it right on his boss's jacket above his heart. As he gave him the last extra ribbon, he said, "Would you do me a favor? Would you take this extra ribbon and pass it on by honoring somebody else? The young boy who first gave me the ribbons is doing a project in school and we want to keep this recognition ceremony going and find out how it affects people."

That night the boss came home to his 14-year-old son and sat him down. He said, "The most incredible thing happened to me today. I was in my office and one of the junior executives came in and told me he admired me and gave me a blue ribbon for being a creative genius. Imagine. He thinks I'm a creative genius. Then he put this blue ribbon that says 'Who I Am Makes A Difference' on my jacket above my heart. He gave me an extra ribbon and asked me to find somebody else to honor. As I was driving home tonight, I started thinking about whom I would honor with this ribbon and I thought about you. I want to honor you. My days are really hectic and when I come home I don't pay a lot of attention to you. Sometimes I scream at you for not getting good enough grades in school and for your bedroom being a mess, but somehow tonight, I just wanted to sit here and, well, just let you know that you do make a difference to me. Besides your mother, you are the most important person in my life. You're a great kid and I love you!"

The startled boy started to sob and sob, and he couldn't stop crying. His whole body shook. He looked up at his father and said through his tears, "I was planning on committing suicide tomorrow, Dad, because I didn't think you loved me. Now I don't need to."

—Author Unknown

♦

LOVE SOUGHT IS GOOD, BUT
GIVEN UNSOUGHT IS BETTER.

~ WILLIAM SHAKESPEARE

WITHOUT LOVE,
BENEVOLENCE BECOMES EGOTISM.

~ DR. MARTIN LUTHER KING, JR.

*So now I am giving you
a new commandment:
Love each other.
Just as I have loved you,
you should love each other.*

JOHN 13:34 NLT

*But the fruit of the Spirit is love,
joy, peace, longsuffering, kindness,
goodness, faithfulness, gentleness
and self-control.*

GALATIANS 5:22, 23 NKJV

JESUS' EXTRAVAGANT *Love* IS FULL OF COMPASSION

He felt compassion for her...

LUKE 7:13 NASB

HE CHOOSES HIS OWN!

Christ chooses his own from the beginning; 2
Thessalonians 2:13: "But we are bound to give thanks
always to God for you, brethren, beloved of the Lord,
because God hath from the beginning chosen you to salvation
through sanctification of the Spirit, and belief of the truth," Eph. 1:4,
"According as he had chosen us in him before the foundation of the
world, that we should be holy and without blame before him in
love." So, brethren, it was before the foundation of the world that
Christ chose his own; when there was neither sun nor moon; when
there was neither sea nor land—it was from the beginning. Ah, he
might well say, you have not chosen me. It was before man loved
man, or angel loved angel, that Christ chose his own. Now, I know
the meaning of Paul when he says, That you may be able to know
the length and breadth, the height and the depth of the love of Christ,
which passeth knowledge. Now, I am not surprised at the death of
Christ! It was a love so great that it broke over the banks that held
it in; a love that broke over a Calvary and a Gethsemane. O
brethren! Do you know this love? Why did he choose me? I
answer, that the reason why he choose you was, the good pleasure
of his will....You will see this illustrated in Mark 3:13, "And he goeth

up into a mountain, and calleth unto him whom he would: and they came unto him." There was a great crowd round about him; he called some, he did not call all. The reason here given why he did it is, "He called whom he would." There is no reason in the creature; the reason is in him who chooses. You will see this in Malachi 1:2: "I have loved you, saith the Lord; yet ye say, Wherein hast thou loved us? Was not Esau Jacob's brother? Saith the Lord: yet I loved Jacob, and I hated Esau." Were they not of the same mother? Yet I loved Jacob, and I hated Esau. The only reason given, you see, is, "I will have mercy on whom I will have mercy." You will see this also in Romans 9:15, 16. The only reason given in the Bible why Christ loved us—and if you study till you die you will not find another—is, "I will have mercy on whom I will have mercy." This is evident from all those that Christ chooses. We read of two great apostacies —one on earth, the other in heaven. First of all, one in heaven; Lucifer, the son of the morning, through pride, sinned, and God cast him, and those that sinned with him, into hell. The second was on earth; Adam sinned, and was driven out of paradise. They were both deserving of punishment. God had a purpose of love; which is it for? Perhaps angels pleaded for their fellow-angels; yet Christ passed them by, and died for man. Why did he die for man? The answer is, "I will have mercy on whom I will have mercy." The same thing is evident in the individuals Christ chooses. You would think Christ would choose the rich, and yet what says James? "Hath not God chosen the poor of this world, rich in faith, and heirs of the kingdom, which he hath promised to them that love him?" Again, you would think Christ would choose the noble; they have not the prejudices that the poor have; but what says the Scripture, "Not many rich, not many noble are called." Again, you would think he would choose those that are learned. The Bible is written in difficult language; its doctrines are hard to be understood; yet what says Christ? "I thank thee, O Father, that thou hast hid these things from the wise and prudent, and hast revealed them unto babes." Again, you would think he would have chosen the virtuous. Though there are nonerighteous, yet there are some more virtuous than others; yet what says Christ? The publicans and the harlots enter the kingdom of heaven while the Pharisee is shut out. "O the depth both of the riches and knowledge of God! How un-searchable are his judgments, and his ways past finding out!" Why did he take the most vile? Here is the only reason I have been able to find ever since I read my Bible—I will have mercy on whom I will have mercy, and I will have compassion on whom I will have compassion." —R. M. McCheney

But whoever has the world's goods, and sees his brother in need and closes his heart against him, how does the love of God abide in him?

I JOHN 3:17 NASB

LOVE IS NOT SOMETHING YOU FEEL. IT'S SOMETHING YOU DO.

DAVID WILKERSON

*J*esus, lover of my soul, I cry out to You today to help me to be a more sensitive and compassionate person. I pray that I will fill my heart with so much of Your Word that the right, and thereby, purest, thoughts and emotions will flow out of me to my family, my friends, and to those I meet along the way. Oh, Dear Jesus, help me to show genuine compassion and love as I live out this Christian life here on earth. I pray that I will be the sweet aroma of Christ Jesus as I represent You, Lord. *Amen*

LOVE IN THE HOME

If I live in a house of spotless beauty with everything in its place,
but have not love, I am a housekeeper—not a homemaker.
If I have time for waxing, polishing, and decorative achievements,
but have not love, my children learn cleanliness—not godliness.
Love leaves the dust in search of a child's laugh.
Love smiles at the tiny fingerprints on a newly cleaned window.
Love wipes away the tears before it wipes up the spilled milk.
Love picks up the child before it picks up the toys.
Love is present through the trials.
Love reprimands, reproves, and is responsive.
Love crawls with the baby, walks with the toddler, runs with the
child, then stands aside to let the youth walk into adulthood.
Love is the key that opens salvation's message to a child's heart.
Before I became a mother I took glory in my house of perfection.
Now I glory in God's perfection of my child. As a mother, there is
much I must teach my child, but the greatest of all is love.

~ AUTHOR UNKNOWN

JESUS' EXTRAVAGANT *Love* IS PROFOUND

*See how great a love the Father
has bestowed upon us, that we
should be called children of God ...*

I JOHN 3:1 NASB

PROFOUND LOVE

I t is during our deepest, darkest times that we can feel most alone. It is also when the love of Jesus can become most profound. Mine came at a time in my life when, by the world's standard, I should have been at my happiest. My husband and I had just completed our second adoption of beautiful, physically healthy children. Yet I knew in my heart that something wasn't right.

Our oldest son, adopted from Haiti when he was 16 months old, was a very angry, just turned 5-year-old. He refused any and all correction and had even tried to hurt his 11-month-old brother. This turned into violence on his part as we tried to love him the best we knew how. He would kick, hit, throw heavy things, pull my hair, and spit on me. He had put holes in his bedroom walls and had even put his fingers in light sockets "to make them tingle." As the months of fights and violence went on, the prayers got stronger. My husband and I were on our knees almost constantly wondering what to do and what was in store for us.

It was during one particularly hard night when my husband and I were kneeling by our bed crying out to Jesus that I found myself complaining to Him. "Jesus, what am I supposed to do?" It was then that He softly said to my heart, "I endured all of those things and more for you because I love you." It was not that Jesus wanted me to endure any of what He had to endure on the cross. He did all of this in my life for me to really show how much He loves me. He was showing me just how much He loved me through my relationship with my precious son, His gift to my husband and me. Thank you, loving Jesus. —Marcia Russell

◆

Love never gives up, never loses faith, is always hopeful, and endures through every circumstance.

I CORINTHIANS 13:7 NLT

◆

Let us not lose heart in doing good, for in due time we will reap if we do not grow weary.

GALATIANS 6:9 NASB

◆

And walk in love, just as Christ also loved you and gave Himself up for us, an offering and a sacrifice to God as a fragrant aroma.

EPHESIANS 5:2 NASB

*If you keep My commandments, you will abide
in My love, just as I have kept My Father's
commandments and abide in His love.*

JOHN 15:10 NKJV

◆

DO YOU KNOW JESUS?

Do you know Jesus?

Do you know Jesus?

Do you know Jesus,

And the wonder of His love?

Yes, I know Jesus!

Yes, I know Jesus!

Yes, I know Jesus,

And the wonder of His love!

~WILLIAM MCGINNIS

The Bible tells us that, "You are loved with an everlasting love." There is nothing superficial about the way Jesus loves His children. His love never stops. Often we pick at things until confusion clouds our thinking, but what the Lord said is the final word on the matter and He said, "You are loved with an everlasting love!" Everything we do as Christians should be as unto the Lord Jesus, because without Him we are lost and doomed for eternity away from all that He has gone to prepare for us in Heaven. His message is simple, but profound. He paid the full price for us...He gave His life...if that isn't love, if that isn't love...but, it is! Profound love!

❖

*T*hank You, Jesus, for the profoundness of Your Word, of Your life, and of what is ours when we leave this world, when we have accepted You as our Lord and Savior. How wonderfully blessed we are and how thankful we are to You, Jesus, precious Jesus. *Amen*

JESUS' EXTRAVAGANT *Love* IS THE HIGHEST ...AGAPE

... He stayed ...

JOHN 11:6 NKJV

AGAPE LOVE

"As the Father has loved me so I have loved you," and "This is my commandment: love one another as I have loved you" John 15:12. Jesus is talking of a very special kind of love, love that does not think of oneself, but sacrifices for the sake of the other. To make sure we would not confuse this very special type of love with other types of love, which often are more lust than love, the writers of the New Testament used a very special word to describe the love of Jesus for us and the love of God for us. They said Jesus loved us with agape love—that is love that does not think of oneself but sacrifices for the sake of the other. Jesus is our model for loving with this sacrificial love, agape love, loving the other for their benefit without putting ourselves first. When does Jesus show us that agape love most of all? When he died on the cross...for us. That is why in our Gospel today Jesus also says, "A man can have no greater love than to lay down his life for his friends" John 15:13. So, let us love one another since love comes from God and anyone who fails to love can never have known God because, "God is love." —Tommy Lane

As the Father hath loved me,
so have I loved you:
continue ye in my love.

JOHN 15:9 KJV

❖

This is My commandment, that you love one another,
just as I have loved you.

JOHN 15:12 NASB

❖

THE GREATEST HAPPINESS IN LIFE IS THE CONVICTION

THAT WE ARE LOVED—LOVED FOR OURSELVES,

OR RATHER, LOVED IN SPITE OF OURSELVES.

~VICTOR HUGO

I LOVE YOU MY CHILD
(Hebrew 13:5)

I saw the tears you shed today
Your heart was grieved and in such pain
Listen child I'm here for you
I'll never ever abandon you

Satan's sifting you like sand
Wants to destroy the life I planned
But I have a hold of you
Don't worry child, I'll see you through

Just cling to me there's victory
In my time child, you will see
The test you're deep within today
Isn't here, my child, to stay

I love you child more than you know
I'll tell and tell and tell you so
You know you mean so much to me
I sent My Child to Calvary

So come up here my little one
Your Father's gripping you with love
Let me wipe your tears away
Hold on My sweet one, another day

–LINDA SMITH

Tender love of Jesus, so lovely and so pure;
Flowing thru this vessel to strengthen, fill and cure
All the doubt and turmoil that's caused by sin and shame,
Making me a witness to His most holy Name.
Yes, love, Christ's love, pure love, great love;
With joy my heart is singing, the things of life grow dim,
For Christ is love!

Thru the passing ages flowed down this love divine,
Lighting men and angels and causing them to shine,
What a heav'nly radiance, His glory from above,
Sunshine of the Spirit, the holy light of love.
Yes, love, Christ's love, pure love, great love;
With joy my heart is singing, the things of life grow dim,
For Christ is love!

Tender love from Heaven in Jesus came to live,

Showing us how God loves, and then His life to give;

Came to be a servant, with God's great pow'r and peace

Leads us to the Father, Whose love will never cease.

God's love, sweet love from Heav'n above.

This love is like an ocean, its waves are reaching me;

Christ came this love to be.

Love is mine in Jesus, this Babe of Bethlehem,

Prince of Peace forever, the Christ, the great I Am.

Angels gave the message, and shepherds passed it on,

Love will be the story when Heav'n and earth are gone.

God's love, sweet love from Heav'n above.

This love is like an ocean, its waves are reaching me;

Christ came this love to be.

~ RUTH EMSWILER

*J*esus, one attribute of the Fruit of the
Spirit is Agape Love. Such an anointing
of the highest form of love upon us
humbles us before You. Thank You, dear
and loving Jesus. *Amen*

JESUS, LOVER OF MY SOUL

Jesus, lover of my soul, let me to thy bosom fly,
while the nearer waters roll, while the tempest still is high.
Hide me, O my Savior, hide, till the storm of life
is past; safe into the haven guide; O receive my soul at last.
Other refuge have I none, hangs my helpless soul on thee;
leave, ah! Leave me not alone, still support and comfort me.
All my trust on thee is stayed, all my help from thee I bring;
cover my defenseless head with the shadow of thy wing.
Thou, O Christ, art all I want, more than all in thee I find;
raise the fallen, cheer the faint, heal the sick, and lead the blind.
Just and holy is thy name, I am all unrighteousness;
false and full of sin I am; thou art full of truth and grace.
Plenteous grace with thee is found, grace to cover all my sin;
let the healing streams abound, make and keep me pure within.
Thou of life the fountain art, freely let me take of thee;
spring thou up within my heart; rise to all eternity.

~ CHARLES WESLEY

JESUS' EXTRAVAGANT *Love* LOOKS AT THE HEART

Blessed are the pure in heart,
for they shall see God.

MATTHEW 5:8 NASB

A MOTHER'S HEART

D uring our [civil] war, there was a Southern man who
came over to a Wisconsin regiment, saying he could not
fight to uphold slavery. Some time after, the mail from the
north came in, and all the men got letters from their relations, and
universal joy prevailed. This Southern man said he wished he were
dead; he was most unhappy, for there were no letters for him. His
mother was dead, and his father and brothers would have shot him
if they could, for going against them. This man's tent-mate was very
sorry for his friend, and when he wrote to his mother in
Wisconsin, he just told her all about it. His mother sat down and
wrote to her son's friend. She called him her son, and spoke to him
like a mother. She told him when the war was over that he must
come to her, and that her home would be his. When the letter
reached the regiment, the chaplain took it down to where this man
was standing, and told him it was for him; but he said it was a
mistake, that nobody would write to him; he had no friends, it must
be for someone else. He was persuaded to open it, and when he
read it, he felt such joy. He went down the lines, saying, "I've got a
mother!" When afterwards the regiment was disbanded, and the
men were returning to their homes, there was none who showed so

much anxiety as this man to get to his mother in Wisconsin. If blessings don't come this week, they will come the next, only persevere. Be of good courage, Christ will strengthen your heart.

— Dwight L. Moody

TO LOVE AT ALL IS TO BE VULNERABLE.
LOVE ANYTHING AND YOUR HEART WILL
CERTAINLY BE WRUNG AND PROBABLY BROKEN.
IF YOU WANT TO MAKE SURE OF
KEEPING INTACT, YOU MUST GIVE YOUR HEART
TO NO ONE, NOT EVEN AN ANIMAL.
WRAP IT CAREFULLY AROUND WITH HOBBIES
AND LITTLE LUXURIES; AVOID ALL
ENTANGLEMENTS, LOCK IT UP SAFELY
IN THE CASKET OF YOUR SELFISHNESS.
BUT IN THAT CASKET—SAFE, DARK, MOTIONLESS,
AIRLESS—IT WILL CHANGE.
IT WILL NOT BE BROKEN; IT WILL BECOME
IMPENETRABLE, IRREDEEMABLE...THE ONLY PLACE
OUTSIDE HEAVEN WHERE YOU CAN BE PERFECTLY
SAFE FROM ALL THE DANGER OF LOVE, IS HELL.

~ C. S. LEWIS

Above all, love each other deeply,
Because love covers a multitude of sins.

✦

O PERFECT LIFE OF LOVE

O perfect life of love! All, all, is finished now,

All that He left His throne above to do for us below.

No work is left undone of all the Father willed;

His toil, His sorrows, one by one, the Scriptures have fulfilled.

No pain that we can share but He has felt its smart;

All forms of human grief and care have pierced that tender heart.

And on His thorn-crowned head and on His sinless soul

Our sins in all that guilt were laid that He might make us whole.

In perfect love He dies; for me He dies, for me.

O all-atoning Sacrifice, I cling by faith to Thee.

In every time of need, before the judgment-throne,

Thy works, O Lamb of God, I'll plead, Thy merits, not mine own.

Yet work, O Lord, in me as Thou for me hast wrought,

And let my love the answer be to grace Thy love has brought.

~ HENRY W. BAKER

EVERYBODY CAN BE GREAT BECAUSE ANYBODY CAN SERVE.

YOU DON'T HAVE TO HAVE COLLEGE DEGREE TO SERVE.

YOU DON'T HAVE TO MAKE YOUR

SUBJECT AND VERB AGREE TO SERVE.

YOU ONLY NEED A HEART FULL OF GRACE.

A SOUL GENERATED BY LOVE.

~ DR. MARTIN LUTHER KING, JR.

Sweet Jesus, it is Your Father's heart that desires to give to us a place called home, a home filled with Your love and open arms. Thank You, Jesus, for such a great love. Thank You, too, that we can express Your love through the many opportunities that You bring to our attention every day. Help us, we pray, to hear what You are saying, and to act according to Your leading. *Amen*

HOLY, HOLY, HOLY!

Holy, holy, holy!
Though the darkness hide Thee,
Though the eye of sinful man
Thy glory may not see,
Only Thou art holy!
There is none beside Thee,
Perfect in pow'r, in
Love and purity.

~ REGINALD HEBER

JESUS' EXTRAVAGANT *Love* SHELTERS

I am the good shepherd;
the good shepherd lays down
His life for the sheep.

JOHN 10:11 NASB

THE SAFEST SHELTER

Who this Man is we all know? Who could He be but the Second Man, the LORD from heaven, the man of sorrows, the Son of Man? What a hiding place He has been to His people! He bears the full force of the wind Himself, and so He shelters those who hide themselves in Him. We have thus escaped the wrath of God, and we shall thus escape the anger of men, the cares of this life, and the dread of death. Why do we stand in the wind when we may so readily and so surely get out of it by hiding behind our LORD? Let us this day run to Him and be at peace. Often the common wind of trouble rises in its force and becomes a tempest, sweeping everything before it. Things which looked firm and stable rock in the blast, and many and great are the falls among our carnal confidences. Our LORD Jesus, the glorious man, is a covert which is never blown down. In Him we mark the tempest sweeping by, but we ourselves rest in delightful serenity. This day let us just stow ourselves away in our hiding place and sit and sing under the protection of our Covert. Blessed Jesus! Blessed Jesus! How we love Thee! Well we may, for Thou art to us a shelter in the time of storm. —C.H. Spurgeon

If ye keep My Commandments,
ye shall abide in My love.

JOHN 15:10 KJV

✦

He shall cover thee with his feathers,
and under his wings shalt thou trust.

PSALMS 91:4 KJV

✦

And now abide faith, hope, love, these three;
but the greatest of these is love.

I CORINTHIANS 13:13 NKJV

✦

LOVE IS ETERNAL—THE ASPECT MAY CHANGE, BUT NOT THE ESSENCE.
THERE IS THE SAME DIFFERENCE IN A PERSON BEFORE AND AFTER HE
IS IN LOVE AS THERE IS IN AN UNLIGHTED LAMP AND ONE THAT IS
BURNING. THE LAMP WAS THERE AND WAS A GOOD LAMP, BUT NOW
IT IS SHEDDING LIGHT TOO, AND THAT IS ITS REAL FUNCTION. AND
LOVE MAKES ONE CALMER ABOUT MANY THINGS, AND THAT WAY,
ONE IS MORE FIT FOR ONE'S WORK.

~ VINCENT VAN GOGH

THROUGH THE STORMS

I did not know His love before, the way I know it now.

I could not see my need for Him, my pride would not allow.

I had it all, without a care, the "Self-sufficient" lie.

My path was smooth, my sea was still, not a cloud was in my sky.

I thought I knew His love for me, I thought I'd seen His grace,

I thought I did not need to grow, I thought I'd found my place.

But then the way grew rough and dark, the storm clouds quickly rolled;

The waves began to rock my ship, my anchor would not hold.

The ship that I had built myself was made of foolish pride.

It fell apart and left me bare, with nowhere else to hide.

I had no strength or faith to face the trials that lay ahead,

And so I simply prayed to Him and bowed my weary head.

His loving arms enveloped me, and then He helped me stand.

He said, "You still must face this storm, but I will hold your hand."

So through the dark and lonely night He guided me through pain.

I could not see the light of day or when the storm might wane.

Yet through the aches and endless tears, my faith began to grow.

I could not see it at the time, but my light began to glow.

I saw God's love in brand new light, His grace and mercy, too.

For only when all self was gone could Jesus' love shine through.

It was not easy in the storm, I sometimes wondered, "Why?"

At times I thought, "I can't go on." I'd hurt, and doubt, and cry.

But Jesus never left my side, He guided me each day.

Through pain and strife, through fire and flood, He helped me all the way.

And now I see as never before how great His love can be.

How in my weakness He is strong, how Jesus cares for me!

He worked it all out for my good, although the way was rough.

He only sent what I could bear, and then He cried, "Enough!"

He raised His hand and said, "Be still!" He made the storm clouds cease.

He opened up the gates of joy and flooded me with peace.

I saw His face now clearer still, I felt His presence strong,

I found anew His faithfulness, He never did me wrong.

Now I know more storms will come, but only for my good,

For pain and tears have helped me grow as naught else ever could.

I still have so much more to learn as Jesus works in me;

If in the storm I'll love Him more, that's where I want to be!

~AUTHOR UNKNOWN

SAFE IN THE ARMS OF JESUS

Safe in the arms of Jesus,

Safe on His gentle breast,

There by His love o'ershadowed, sweetly my soul shall rest.

Hark! 'Tis the voice of angels, borne in a song to me,

Over the fields of glory, over the jasper sea.

Safe in the arms of Jesus,

Safe from corroding care,

Safe from the world's temptations, sin cannot harm me there.

Free from the blight of sorrow, free from my doubts and fears;

Only a few more trials, only a few more tears!

Jesus, my heart's dear refuge,

Jesus has died for me;

Firm on the Rock of Ages, ever my trust shall be.

Here let me wait with patience, wait till the night is o'er;

Wait till I see the morning break on the golden shore.

~ FANNY J. CROSBY

JESUS' EXTRAVAGANT *Love* IS ACTIVE

*I have made Your name known
to them, and will make it known,
so that the love with which You loved
Me may be in them, and I in them.*

JOHN 17:26 NASB

8-2-15

STILL HE WALKED

He could hear the crowds screaming "crucify, crucify." He could hear the hatred in their voices, these were His chosen people. He loved them, and they were going to crucify Him. He was beaten, bleeding and weakened...His heart was broken, but still He walked. He could see the crowd as He came from the palace. He knew each of their faces so well. He had created them. He knew every smile, laugh, and shed tear, but now they were contorted with rage and anger...His heart broke, but still He walked. Was he scared? You and I would have been, so His humanness would have mandated that He was. He felt alone. His disciples had left, denied, and even betrayed Him. He searched the crowd for a loving face and He saw very few. Then He turned His eyes to the only one that mattered and He knew that He would never be alone. He looked back at the crowd, at the people who were spitting at Him, throwing rocks at Him and mocking Him and He knew that because of Him, they would never be alone. So for them, He walked. The sounds of the hammer striking the spikes echoed through the crowd. The sounds of His cries echoed even louder. The cheers of the crowd, as His hands and feet were nailed to the cross, intensified with each blow. Loudest of all was the still small voice inside His Heart that whispered, "I am with you, my Son", and

God's heart broke. He had let His Son walk. Jesus could have asked God to end His suffering, but instead He asked God to forgive. Not to forgive Him, but to forgive the ones who were persecuting Him. As He hung on that cross, dying an unimaginable death, He looked out and saw, not only the faces in the crowd, but also, the face of every person yet to be, and His heart filled with love. As His body was dying, His heart was alive. Alive with the limitless, unconditional love He feels for each of us. That is why He walked. When I forget how much my God loves me, I remember His walk. When I wonder if I can be forgiven, I remember His walk. When I need reminding of how to live like Christ, I think of His walk. And to show Him how much I love Him, I wake up each morning, turn my eyes to Jesus, and I walk.

—Author Unknown

But God demonstrates His own love toward us, in that while we were yet sinners, Christ died for us. Much more then, having now been justified by His blood, we shall be saved from the wrath of God through Him. For if while we were enemies we were reconciled to God through the death of His Son, much more, having been reconciled, we shall be saved by His life. And not only this, but we also exult in God through our Lord Jesus Christ, through whom we have now received the reconciliation.

ROMANS 5:8-11 NASB

Alas! And did my Savior bleed, and did my Sovereign die?

Would He devote that sacred head for such a worm as I?

Was it for crimes that I had done, He groaned upon the tree?

Amazing pity grace unknown, and love beyond degree!

Well, might the sun in darkness hide and shut His glories in

When God, the Mighty Maker died, for man and creatures' sins.

Thus might I hide my blushing face

When His dear cross appears,

Dissolve my heart in thankfulness, and melt mine eyes to tears.

But drops of grief can ne're repay the debt of love I owe;

Here, Lord, I give myself away, 'tis all that I can do.

~ ISAAC WATTS

And one of them, a lawyer, asked Him a question, testing Him, "Teacher, which is the great commandment in the law?" And He said to him, "'YOU SHALL LOVE THE LORD YOUR GOD WITH ALL YOUR HEART, AND WITH ALL YOUR SOUL, AND WITH ALL YOUR MIND.'
"This is the great and foremost commandment.
"The second is like it, 'YOU SHALL LOVE YOUR NEIGHBOR AS YOURSELF.'"

MATTHEW 22:35-39 NASB

HOW SWEET THE NAME OF JESUS

How sweet the name of Jesus sounds in a believer's ear!
It soothes his sorrows, heals his wounds, and drives away his fear.
It makes the wounded spirit whole, and calms the troubled breast;
'Tis manna to the hungry soul, and to the weary rest.
Dear name! The Rock on which I build,
my shield, and hiding-place,
My never-failing treasury, filled with boundless stores of grace!
Jesus, my Shepherd, Husband, Friend,
My Prophet, Priest, and King;
My Lord, my Life, my Way, my End, accept the praise I bring.
Weak is the effort of my heart, and cold my warmest thought;
But when I see Thee as Thou art I'll praise Thee as I ought.
Till then I would Thy love proclaim with every fleeting breath;
And may the music of Thy name refresh my soul in death!

~JOHN NEWTON

*L*oving Jesus, You have blessed us with the means for us to know how to live a righteous life with all the benefits that You can bestow upon us. You are active in Your love for Your children and You have promised to never leave us without You and everything we need to survive and live the life You intended. How grateful we are to You for such love. Your love is broader than anything we can imagine. Thank You for love that never leaves nor forsakes us. *Amen*

JESUS' EXTRAVAGANT *Love* COMFORTS

*For just as the sufferings of Christ
are ours in abundance, so also
our comfort is abundant through Christ.*

II CORINTHIANS 1:5 NASB

THANKS FOR THE THORNS

S andra felt as low as the heels of her Birkenstock shoes as she pushed against a November gust and the florist shop door. Her life had been easy, like a Spring breeze. Then in the fourth month of her second pregnancy, a minor Automobile accident stole her ease. During this Thanksgiving week she would have delivered a son. She grieved over her loss. As if that weren't enough her husband's company threatened a transfer. Then her sister, whose holiday visit she coveted, called saying she could not come. What's worse, Sandra's friend infuriated her by suggesting her grief was a God-given path to maturity that would allow her to empathize with others who suffer. "Had she lost a child? No, she has no idea what I'm feeling," Sandra shuddered. "Thanksgiving? Thankful for what?" she wondered. For a careless driver whose truck was hardly scratched when he rear-ended her? For an airbag that saved her life but took that of her child?

"Good afternoon, can I help you?" The flower shop clerk's approach startled her. "Sorry," said the clerk, Jenny, "I just didn't want you to think I was ignoring you."

"I...I need an arrangement."

"For Thanksgiving?" Sandra nodded. "Do you want beautiful

but ordinary, or would you like to challenge the day with a customer favorite I call the Thanksgiving Special?" Jenny saw Sandra's curiosity and continued. "I'm convinced that flowers tell stories, that each arrangement insinuates a particular feeling. Are you looking for something that conveys gratitude this Thanksgiving?"

"Not exactly!" Sandra blurted. "Sorry, but in the last five months, everything that could go wrong has."

Sandra regretted her outburst but was surprised when Jenny said, "I have the perfect arrangement for you." The door's small bell suddenly rang. "Barbara! Hi," Jenny said. She politely excused herself from Sandra and walked toward a small workroom. She quickly reappeared carrying a massive arrangement of greenery, bows, and long-stemmed thorny roses. Only, the ends of the rose stems were neatly snipped, no flowers.

"Want this in a box?" Jenny asked. Sandra watched for Barbara's response. Was this a joke? Who would want rose stems and no flowers! She waited for laughter, for someone to notice the absence of flowers atop the thorny stems, but neither woman did.

"Yes, please. It's exquisite," said Barbara. "You'd think after three years of getting the special, I'd not be so moved by its significance, but it's happening again. My family will love this one. Thanks." Sandra stared. Why so normal a conversation about so strange an arrangement? she wondered.

"Ah. . ." said Sandra, pointing. "That lady just left with, ah. . ."

"Yes?"

"Well, she had no flowers!"

"Right, I cut off the flowers."

"Off?"

"Off. Yep. That's the Special. I call it the Thanksgiving Thorns Bouquet."

"But, why do people pay for that?" In spite of herself she chuckled.

"Do you really want to know?"

"I couldn't leave this shop without knowing. I'd think about nothing else!"

"That might be good," said Jenny. "Well," she continued, "Barbara came into the shop three years ago feeling very much like you feel today. She thought she had very little to be thankful for. She had lost her father to cancer, the family business was failing, her son was into drugs, and she faced major surgery."

"Ouch!" said Sandra.

"That same year, I lost my husband. I assumed complete responsibility for the shop and for the first time, spent the holidays alone. I had no children, no husband, no family nearby, and too great a debt to allow any travel."

"What did you do?"

"I learned to be thankful for thorns."

Sandra's eyebrows lifted. "Thorns?"

"I'm a Christian, Sandra. I've always thanked God for good things in life and I never thought to ask Him why good things happened to me. But, when bad stuff hit, did I ever ask! It took time to learn that dark times are important. I always enjoyed the 'flowers' of life but it took thorns to show me the beauty of God's comfort. You know, the Bible says that God comforts us when we're afflicted and from His consolation we learn to comfort others."

Sandra gasped. "A friend read that passage to me and I was furious! I guess the truth is I don't want comfort. I've lost a baby and I'm angry with God." She started to ask Jenny to "go on" when the door's bell diverted their attention.

"Hey, Phil!" shouted Jenny as a balding, rotund man entered the shop. She softly touched Sandra's arm and moved to welcome him. He tucked her under his arm at his side for a warm hug.

"I'm here for twelve thorny long-stemmed stems!" Phil laughed, heartily.

"I figured as much," said Jenny. "I've got them ready." She lifted a tissue-wrapped arrangement from the refrigerated cabinet.

"Beautiful," said Phil. "My wife will love them."

Sandra could not resist asking. "These are for your wife?" Phil saw that Sandra's curiosity matched his when he first heard of a Thorn Bouquet. "Do you mind me asking, "Why thorns?"

"In fact, I'm glad you asked," he said. "Four years ago my wife and I nearly divorced. After forty years, we were in a real mess, but we slogged through, problem by rotten problem. We rescued our marriage, our love, really. Last year at Thanksgiving I stopped in here for flowers. I must have mentioned surviving a tough process because Jenny told me that for a long time she kept a vase of rose stems—stems as a reminder of what she learned from "thorny" times. That was good enough for me. I took home stems. My wife and I decided to label each one for a specific thorny situation and give thanks for what the problem taught us. I'm pretty sure this stem review is becoming a tradition." Phil paid Jenny, thanked her again and as he left, said to Sandra, "I highly recommend the Special!"

"I don't know if I can be thankful for the thorns in my life," Sandra said to Jenny.

"Well, my experience says that thorns make roses more precious. We treasure God's providential care more during trouble than at any other time. Remember, Sandra, Jesus wore a crown of thorns so that we might know His love. Do not resent thorns." Tears rolled down Sandra's cheeks. For the first time since the accident she loosened her grip on resentment. "I'll take twelve long-stemmed thorns, please."

"I hoped you would," Jenny said. "I'll have them ready in a minute. Then, every time you see them, remember to appreciate both good and hard times. We grow through both."

"Thank you. What do I owe you?"

"Nothing. Nothing but a pledge to work toward healing your heart. The first year's arrangement is always on me." Jenny handed a card to Sandra. "I'll attach a card like this to your arrangement but maybe you'd like to read it first. Go ahead, read it."

"My God, I have never thanked Thee for my thorn! I have thanked Thee a thousand times for my roses, but never once for my thorn. Teach me the glory of the cross I bear, teach me the value of my thorns. Show me that I have climbed to Thee by the path of pain. Show me that my tears have made my rainbow—George Matheson."

Jenny said, "Happy Thanksgiving, Sandra," handing her the Special. "I look forward to our knowing each other better." Sandra smiled. She turned, opened the door, and walked toward hope! Jesus endured the thorns of Calvary pressing into the very skin on His head, to show how much He loves us. How important it is for us to remember the extravagance of His love when we find ourselves depressed and despondent about the thorns of life. —Author Unknown

JESUS' EXTRAVAGANT *Love* IS FULL OF GRACE

He gives a greater grace.

JAMES 4:6 NASB

FULL OF GRACE

11-1-15

One day, I woke early in the morning to watch the sunrise. Ah, the beauty of God's creation is beyond description. As I watched, I praised God for His beautiful work. As I sat there, I felt the Lord's presence with me. He asked me, "Do you love me?"

I answered, "Of course, God! You are my Lord and Savior!"

Then He asked, "If you were physically handicapped, would you still love me?"

I was perplexed. I looked down upon my arms, legs and the rest of my body and wondered how many things I wouldn't be able to do, the things that I took for granted. And I answered, "It would be tough Lord, but I would still love You."

Then the Lord said, "If you were blind, would you still love my creation?"

How could I love something without being able to see it? Then I thought of all the blind people in the world and how many of them still loved God and His creation. So I answered, "Its hard to think of it, but I would still love you."

The Lord then asked me, "If you were deaf, would you still listen to my word?"

How could I listen to anything being deaf? Then I understood. Listening to God's Word is not merely using our ears, but our hearts. I answered, "It would be tough, but I would still listen to Your word."

The Lord then asked, "If you were mute, would you still praise My Name?"

How could I praise without a voice? Then it occurred to me: God wants us to sing from our very heart and soul. It never matters what we sound like. And praising God is not always with a song, but when we are persecuted, we give God praise with our words of thanks. So I answered, "Though I could not physically sing, I would still praise Your Name."

And the Lord asked, "Do you really love Me?"

With courage and a strong conviction, I answered boldly, "Yes Lord! I love You because You are the one and true God!"

I thought I had answered well, but God asked, "THEN WHY DO YOU SIN?"

I answered, "Because I am only human. I am not perfect."

"THEN WHY IN TIMES OF PEACE DO YOU STRAY THE FURTHEST? WHY ONLY IN TIMES OF TROUBLE DO YOU PRAY THE EARNEST?" No answers. Only tears. The Lord continued: "Why only sing at fellowships and retreats? Why seek Me only in times of worship? Why ask things so selfishly? Why ask things so unfaithfully?" The tears continued to roll down my cheeks. "Why are you ashamed of Me? Why are you not spreading the good news? Why in times of persecution, you cry to others when I offer My shoulder to cry on? Why make excuses when I give you opportunities to serve in My Name?" I tried to answer, but there was no answer to give. "You are blessed with life. I made you not to throw this gift away. I have blessed you with talents to serve Me, but you continue to turn away. I have revealed My Word to you, but you do not gain in knowledge. I have spoken to you but your ears were closed. I have shown My blessings to you, but your eyes were turned away. I have sent you servants, but you sat idly by as they were pushed away. I have heard your prayers and I have answered them all. DO YOU TRULY LOVE ME?"

I could not answer. How could I? I was embarrassed beyond belief. I had no excuse. What could I say to this? When the tears had flowed,

I said, "Please forgive me Lord. I am unworthy to be Your child."

The Lord answered, "That is My Grace, My child."

I asked, "Then why do you continue to forgive me? Why do You love me so?"

The Lord answered, "Because you are My creation. You are my child. I will never abandon you. When you cry, I will have compassion and cry with you. When you shout with joy, I will laugh with you. When you are down, I will encourage you. When you fall, I will raise you up. When you are tired, I will carry you. I will be with you till the end of days, and I will love you forever."

Never had I cried so hard before. How could I have been so cold? How could I have hurt God as I had done? I asked God, "How much do You love me?" The Lord stretched out His arms, and I saw His nail-pierced hands. I bowed down at the feet of Christ, my Savior. And for the first time, I truly prayed. —Anon

◆

THE SCRIPTURAL IDEA OF GRACE IS LOVE THAT STOOPS,
AND THAT PARDONS, AND THAT COMMUNICATES.

~ ALEXANDER MACLAREN

◆

This is my comfort in my affliction,
For Your word has given me life.

PSALMS 119:59 NKJV

AMAZING GRACE!

Amazing Grace! How sweet the sound!
That saved a wretch like me!
I once was lost, but now am found was blind but now I see.

'Twas grace that taught my heart to fear.
And grace my fears relieved;
How precious did that grace appear the hour I first believed!

Through many dangers, toils and snares I have already come.
'Tis grace hath brought me safe thus far,
and grace will lead me home!

The Lord has promised good to me,
His word my hope secures;
He will my shield and portion be, as long as life endures.

Yes, when this flesh and heart shall fail, and mortal life shall cease;
I shall possess within the vail, a life of joy and peace!

The earth shall soon dissolve like snow, the sun forbear to shine;
But God who called me here below shall be forever mine!

In evil long I took delight unawed by shame or fear;
'Til a new object met my sight, and stopped my wild career.

I saw One hanging on a tree, in agonies and blood;
Who fixed His languid eyes on me as near His cross I stood.

Sure, never 'til my latest breath, can I forget that look
It seemed to charge me with His death though not a word He spoke.

My conscience owned and felt the guilt, and plunged me in despair;
I saw my sins His blood had shed, and helped to nail Him there.

Alas, I knew not what I did, but all my tears were vain;
Where could my trembling soul be hid, for I the Lord had slain!

When we've been there ten thousand years,
bright shining as the sun;
We've no less days to sing God's praise
than when we first begun!

~JOHN NEWTON

FAIREST LORD JESUS

Fairest Lord Jesus, ruler of all nature,
O Thou of God and man the Son:
Thee will I cherish, thee will I honor,
Thou my soul's glory, joy, and crown.
Fair are the meadows, fairer still the woodlands,
Robed in the blooming garb of spring.
Jesus is fairer, Jesus is purer,
Who makes the woeful heart to sing.
Fair is the sunshine, fairer still the moonlight,
And all the twinkling starry host.
Jesus shines brighter, Jesus shines purer,
Than all the angels heaven can boast.

– AUTHOR UNKNOWN

JESUS' EXTRAVAGANT *Love* IS MIRACULOUS

*Jesus said to them, "Do you believe that
I am able to do this?"*

MATTHEW 9:28 NASB

MAN WITH A PAST

For four years she watched him as he served in the church,
loved his wife and children in the most honoring way,
participated in community activities, and was always ready to
help a neighbor and a friend. He was kind and generous and
everyone loved being in his company. He was a powerful prayer
warrior, and made himself available anytime there was a need in the
church or the community. His Sunday School messages were always
well thought out, very well executed, and people would stand around
afterwards talking about the way his messages touched their lives.
She watched from a distance, from the close relationship she and her
husband had with him and his wife, the way he loved Christ Jesus
and the way Jesus obviously loved him back. His was a beautiful life
to observe.

At a church gathering, a few people were asked to share their
testimony. He was one of the chosen few. It would have been easy
to hear glowing highlights of his Christian background and how he
had come to the Lord Jesus at an early age. Not so! He had only
been saved for one year longer than we had known him. It was not
a vibrant church outreach, not a persistent minister that told him he
was lost and in need of the savior, not parents or a Christian wife

that had burned the night oil praying for him that caused him to repent, confess, and accept the Jesus as His Lord and Savior. No, it was nothing so dramatic that would thrill those listening to him.

He had been in sales and traveled three weeks out of each month, with short breaks in between. His partner traveled with him. Not unlike a lot of men that travel, he made friends with clients in every city he worked and spent his nights partying with them after their business was complete. While he went out night after night to drink and live the 'good life' forgetting about his young wife back home caring for their children, trying to make ends meet, and waiting patiently by the phone, nights on end, for a call from her husband, his partner would return to their hotel room to call his wife, read, spend time with the Lord, and prepare for the next day's business in the field.

Never once did our friend come in before three o'clock in the morning and never once did he come in sober. Not only was he inebriated, but he was loud, rude, nasty, and aggressive. He showed no respect for his partner who was asleep and always awakened. It was a shock to all of us to hear that this kind, gentle, quiet man had been the coarse renegade he was describing.

He went on to tell the group that he was not happy with his life and he knew he was acting like a jerk, especially to his partner.

What caused him to begin to question his lifestyle and to consider that there must be a better one than the one he was leading was his partner. It was the behavior of his partner that caused him to take notice of his own displaced, out-of-order life. His partner never once made a comment to him about his rudeness, never once asked him to be quiet, never once condemned him for coming in just hours before they were to be on the road again, working. He never once said a word about the drinking, the smoking or the nasty language. The partner was always silent.

When the man had his fill, he blurted out to his partner in an abrasive way and begged him to let him in on his secret. Of course, the secret was that the partner was a Christian and he had been praying for his friend for months and he knew God would hear and answer and give him the perfect moment to share the gospel message with him. When the moment came, the partner was ready to give the plan of salvation, and the man was ready to ask for forgiveness and accept Jesus into his life.

From that very day, the man never took another drink, never put another cigarette to his lips, never used another foul word. He surrendered his whole being to the cross of Calvary. Jesus loved him when he did not know it, but Jesus gently prepared the very moment and place where he would throw it all on the line and accept the one his partner served, the person of Jesus. In return, he was transformed and that changed man is what people knew and loved about him. He, in a simple act of obedience to the gospel message, confessed, repented, and accepted the extravagant love of Jesus! —PMH

It is by our actions that we know we are living in the truth, so we will be confident when we stand before the Lord, even if our hearts condemn us. For God is greater than our hearts, and he knows everything.

I JOHN 3:19, 20 NLT

Love is not blind—it simply enables one to see things others fail to see.

~ANONYMOUS

A GIFT OF LOVE

I've nothing else to offer,
So, to you, it's love I'll send,
It's nothing that I borrowed,
And it's nothing that I'd lend.
It has no dollar value,
And it can't be overused;
It isn't fragile, so it can't break,
Though, often it's abused.
I've given it to others,
But each time it's unique,
Its meaning's always different;
It depends on what you seek.
It's something you can store away
To feel when you're in need,
But never is it on display;
Its beauty can't be seen.
I'm giving it "no strings attached,"
No costly warranty;
This love that I am sending
Has a lifetime guarantee.

~ AUTHOR UNKNOWN

JESUS' EXTRAVAGANT *Love* EXTENDS TO CHILDREN

Suffer little children,
and forbid them not,
to come unto me: for of such
is the kingdom of heaven.

MATTHEW 19:13 KJV

IT WAS ALL HE HAD TO GIVE

A nine-year-old boy, from a rural town, lived in a poor area of the community. A nearby church had a bus ministry and the bus pastor knocked on the lad's door one Saturday afternoon. The boy came to answer the door and greeted the pastor. The bus pastor asked if his parents were home and the small boy told him that his parents go off every weekend leaving him at home to take care of his little brother.

The bus pastor couldn't believe what the child was saying and asked him to repeat it. The youngster gave the same answer and the bus pastor asked to come in and talk with him. They went into the living room and sat down on an old couch with foam and springs exposed. The bus pastor asked the boy, "Where do you go to church?"

The young boy surprised the visitor by replying, "I've never been to church in my whole life." The bus pastor thought to himself about the fact that his church was less than three miles from the child's house.

"Are you sure you have never been to church?" he asked again.

"I sure haven't," came his answer. Then the bus pastor said, "Well, son, more important than going to church, have you ever heard the greatest love story ever told?" and then he proceeded to share the Gospel with this little nine year old boy. The young lad's heart began to be tenderized and at the end of the bus pastor's story the bus pastor asked if the boy wanted to receive this free gift from God.

The youngster exclaimed, "You bet!" The kid and the bus pastor got on their knees and the lad invited Jesus into his heart and he received the free gift of salvation. Once they stood, the pastor asked if he could pick both boys up for church the next morning. "Sure," the nine year old replied. The bus pastor arrived at the house early the next morning and found the lights off. He let himself in and worked his way through the house and found the little boys asleep in bed. He woke them up and helped get them dressed. They got on the bus and were treated to a donut for breakfast on their way to church. Never having attended church before and this being a large church gave cause for the boys to sit still and just take things in. They were clueless to what was going on. Minutes into the service several unhappy looking men walked down to the front and picked up some wooden plates. One of the men prayed as the boys sat in utter fascination watching the men mechanically walk up and down the aisles. The oldest boy had no idea what was going on for a long time, then it hit him and he began to understand. These people must be giving money to Jesus. Recalling the free gift of life he had received just twenty-four hours earlier, he immediately searched his pockets, front and back, and couldn't find a thing to give Jesus. By this time the offering plate was being passed down his aisle and with a broken heart he just grabbed the plate and held on to it. He finally let go and watched it pass on down the aisle. Turning around to see the plate passed down the aisle behind him, his eyes were fixed on the plate as it was moved back and forth, back and forth all the way to the rear of the sanctuary. Then he had an idea. The nine-year old boy, in front of God and everybody, rose from his seat, walked about eight rows back, grabbed the usher by the coat, and asked if he could hold the plate one more time. Then he did the most astounding thing when he took the plate, sat it on the floor and stepped into the center of it. As he stood there, he lifted his little head up and said, "Jesus, I don't have anything to give you today, but just me. I give you me!" —Anon

◆

For sin shall not have dominion over you:
for ye are not under the law, but under grace.

ROMANS 6:14 KJV

◆

Behold, children are a heritage from the Lord, The fruit of the womb
is a reward, Like arrows in the hand of a warrior, So are the children
of one's youth. Happy is the man who has his quiver full of them.

PSALMS 127:3-5 NKJV

"For all these things the nations of the world eagerly seek; but your Father knows that you need these things. "But seek His kingdom, and these things will be added to you. "Do not be afraid, little flock, for your Father has chosen gladly to give you the kingdom. "Sell your possessions and give to charity; make yourselves money belts which do not wear out, an unfailing treasure in heaven, where no thief comes near nor moth destroys. "For where your treasure is, there your heart will be also."

LUKE 12:30-34 NASB

❖

Blessed are the pure in heart; for they shall see God.

MATTHEW 5:8 KJV

❖

LOVE SHOULD BE THE SILVER THREAD THAT RUNS THROUGH ALL YOUR CONDUCT. KINDNESS, GENTLENESS, LONG-SUFFERING, FORBEARANCE, PATIENCE, SYMPATHY, A WILLINGNESS TO ENTER INTO CHILDISH TROUBLES, A READINESS TO TAKE PART IN CHILDISH JOYS— THESE ARE THE CORDS BY WHICH A CHILD MAY BE LED MOST EASILY—THESE ARE THE CLUES YOU MUST FOLLOW IF YOU WOULD FIND THE WAY TO HIS HEART.

~J. C. RYLE

JESUS LOVES THE LITTLE CHILDREN

Jesus loves the little children, all the children of the world.

Red and yellow, black and white, they are precious in His sight.

Jesus calls the children dear,

"Come to me and never fear,

For I love the little children of the world;

I will take you by the hand,

Lead you to the better land,

For I love the little children of the world."

Jesus is the Shepherd true,

And He'll always stand by you,

For He loves the little children of the world;

He's a Savior great and strong,

And He'll shield you from the wrong,

For He loves the little children of the world.

I am coming, Lord, to Thee,

And Your soldier I will be,

For You love the little children of the world;

And Your cross I'll always bear,

And for You I'll do and dare,

For You love the little children of the world.

~ C. HERBERT WOOLSTON

SPLINTERS FROM THE CROSS

Little headaches, little heartaches, little griefs of every day,
Little trials and vexations, how they throng around our way!
One great cross, immense and heavy, so it seems to our weak will,
Might be born with resignation, but these many small ones kill.
Yet all life is formed of small things, little leaves make up the trees,
Many tiny drops of water blending, make the mighty seas.
Let us not then by impatience mar the beauty of the whole,
But the love of Jesus bear all in the silence of our soul.
Asking Him for grace sufficient to sustain us through each loss,
And to treasure each small offering as a splinter from His Cross.

~AUTHOR UNKNOWN

❖

*And above all things have fervent love
for one another, for "love will
cover a multitude of sins.*

1 PETER 4:8 NKJV

JESUS' EXTRAVAGANT *Love* IS EXPRESSED THROUGH OTHERS

*To whom God would make known what is the riches
of the glory of this mystery among the Gentiles;
which is Christ in you, the hope of glory.*

COLOSSIANS 1:27 KJV

MRS. DEL

Mrs. Del is a Mother, Grandmother, Great-Grandmother, and a Mother-in-law. I first met her in the early 1970's. I was a longhaired 'left over hippie' from the 60's. Not a great resume for someone wanting to date her only daughter, but I soon learned that Del had a heart bigger than life and a love of the Lord that extended beyond anything I could imagine.

Del was raised in rural North Carolina where she learned of the loving grace of Jesus from her parents. Growing up in the country and marrying young, Del had seen her share of tragedies. Her first husband died of cancer at an early age, leaving Del to raise her three sons by herself. After being a single parent for several years, a career military man, Phil, entered her life and after a short courtship, Phil, though he didn't know about Christianity, married Mrs. Del. Del's patience and her witness led Phil to know the same Jesus that she radiated and, together, they served the Lord Jesus and they were blessed with two more children, one son and one daughter.

After years of traveling with the military, the family settled in Tennessee. This gracious woman opened her doors to many families and individuals and her conversations with them always managed to include telling them about the love of her Savior, Jesus. She had a love relationship with Jesus. He loved her and she loved Him right back.

Tragedy struck again when Del was stricken with a severe stroke. She was never bitter; if anything it gave her more reason to tell everyone she met of the wonderful love of Jesus Christ. The death of a son, who succumbed to cancer in 1994, was the heaviest burden she had to bear.

Through it all, this saint has remained an inspiration and a constant witness of a loving Lord Jesus. Del's outgoing personality and her willingness to share the Word of God with so many friends and strangers is amazing. Del's constant witness and her genuine spirit of kindness is evident as she serves from her chair at home, from her wheelchair at church, and to everyone who is blessed by her prayers for them. When one life comes in contact with another, both are touched. Many will have a glimpse of heaven's rewards because Mrs. Del has touched their lives here on earth. I, included, for I married her daughter and I have experienced the extravagant love of Jesus through both of these committed Christian women.

— Joe Gallagher

*Beloved, do not be surprised at the fiery
ordeal among you, which comes upon you
for your testing, as though some strange
thing were happening to you; but to the degree
that you share the sufferings of Christ, keep
on rejoicing, so that also at the revelation
of His glory you may rejoice with exultation.*

I PETER 4:12, 13 NASB

❖

Great wealth is in the house of the righteous ...

PROVERBS 15:6 NASB

❖

*Serve the LORD with gladness;
Come before Him with joyful singing.*

PSALM 100:2 NASB

❖

They do not love that do not show their love.

~ WILLIAM SHAKESPEARE

LOVE DIVINE, ALL LOVES EXCELLING

Love divine, all loves excelling, joy of heaven, to earth come down;
fix in us thy humble dwelling; all thy faithful mercies crown!
Jesus thou art all compassion, pure, unbounded love thou art;
visit us with thy salvation; enter every trembling heart.

Breathe, O breathe thy loving Spirit into every troubled breast!
Let us all in thee inherit; let us find that second rest.
Take away our bent to sinning; Alpha and Omega be;
end of faith, as its beginning, set our hearts at liberty.

Come, Almighty to deliver, let us all thy life receive;
suddenly return and never, nevermore thy temples leave.
Thee we would be always blessing, serve thee as thy hosts above,
pray and praise thee without ceasing, glory in thy perfect love.

Finish, then, thy new creation; pure and spotless let us be.
Let us see thy great salvation perfectly restored in thee;
changed from glory into glory, till in heaven we take our place,
till we cast our crowns before thee, lost in wonder, love, and praise.

~ CHARLES WESLEY

Loving Jesus, You have given us many brothers and sisters in the Kingdom here on earth. Help us, we pray, to be filled with Your Spirit, speaking to one another in psalms and hymns and spiritual songs, singing and making melodies in our hearts to You, Lord Jesus. May our lives be a living example of You. Lord, the legacy that one so in love with You leaves behind cannot be measured on this earth. *Amen*

JESUS' EXTRAVAGANT *Love* GUIDES US

...he will guide you into all truth...
and he will shew you things to come.

JOHN 16:13 KJV

DECISION MADE IN ADVANCE

The story is told of an elderly man who, a number of years ago had lost his right arm in an accident. At first, the trauma of the loss totally destroyed the man's desire to attend or enter into any sports even though they had been so much a part of his life. All this brought him to severe depression; however, it wasn't long before a caring friend talked him into a game of handball and he was hooked. Amazingly, as fast as his depression came, he lost it. Within a few years he was considered one of the best handball players in his area and had been in numerous tournaments, always doing well and making the game look so easy. In one tournament, he easily won his way into the finals and after making it look so easy, he won the final two games against one of the best players in the game, a man thirty years younger. In an interview with the local newspaper after the match he was asked; "How did you do it?"

To this he replied, "Decisions." Not satisfied with such a simple answer the reporter asked what he meant, "It's easy; every time the ball was hit to my opponent he had to decide which hand to hit it with, however, when the ball was hit to me, it was easy because I had already made my decision." Think about it. What would our lives be like if every time the adversity or Satan himself puts the ball in our 'court' if we had already decided how we would return it? How wonderful if we could always give the answer that, "we have decided for Jesus!" Not unlike the man who gave an account to the media, we would be positioned to give an account to the world that, "Jesus decided for us out of His great love for us so that our decision is made in advance!" — Author Unknown

*J*esus, we look to You for direction
and for making right decisions.
I pray that my decisions will be in
the center of Your will for my life.
I pray that I will position myself so
that I can hear from You the plans
You have for my life. When trials do
come, help me to listen to Your voice
as You speak to my spirit and help
me, dear Jesus, to follow You. *Amen*

Therefore, since we have so great a cloud of witnesses surrounding us, let us also lay aside every encumbrance and the sin which so easily entangles us, and let us run with endurance the race that is set before us, fixing our eyes on Jesus, the author and perfecter of faith, who for the joy set before Him endured the cross, despising the shame, and has sat down at the right hand of the throne of God.

HEBREWS 12:1, 2 NASB

❖

*He knoweth the way that I take:
when he hath tried me,
I shall come forth as gold.*

JOB 23:10 KJV

❖

*Thou shalt remember all the way which
the Lord thy God led thee ...*

DEUTERONOMY 8:2 KJV

POOR, WEAK, AND WORTHLESS, THO' I AM

Poor, weak, and worthless, tho' I am.

I have a rich almighty Friend;

Jesus, the Saviour, is his name,

He freely loves and without end.

He ransomed me from hell with blood,

And by his pow'r my foes controlled;

He found me wand'ring far from God,

And brought me to his chosen fold.

He cheers my heart, my wants supplies,

And says that I shall shortly be

Enthroned with him above the skies;

Oh, what a friend Christ is to me!

~JOHN NEWTON

A new heart also will I give you,
and a new spirit will I put within you:
and I will take away the stony heart out of your flesh,
and I will give you a heart of flesh.

EZEKIEL 36:26 KJV

✦

Listen! The Lord is not too weak to save you, and he
is not becoming deaf. He can hear you when you call.

ISAIAH 59:1 NLT

✦

Jehovah, there is none besides thee to help,
between the mighty and him that hath no strength:
help us, O Jehovah our God; for we rely on thee,
and in thy name are we come against this multitude.
O Jehovah, thou art our God;
let not man prevail against thee.

II CHRONICLES 14:11 ASV

JESUS' EXTRAVAGANT *Love* INTERVENES

...walk in love, just as Christ also
loved you and gave Himself up for us,
an offering and a sacrifice to
God as a fragrant aroma.

EPHESIANS 5:2 NASB

AN EXPRESSION OF LOVE

I was probably six years old, and as usual, had messed up somehow. Mom and dad believed that the shortest way to a child's brain was through the lower end of the spine. So the time had come for the paddle to be applied. What ever I had done must have been pretty bad since the punishment was meant to fit the crime. My older sister, Miriam, had overheard the goings on and knew it was going to be bad.

Now, she was only two years older than I, but she stepped up to mom and dad and told them that she wanted to take my spanking. Mom cried, I rejoiced, and dad delivered the punishment.

It was several years later that it finally dawned on me what Miriam had done. She gave me GRACE. I didn't deserve her gift of deliverance, and she didn't have to give it. The whole episode has stuck with me through the years as a living example of an expression of love, but more importantly to bring reality to the greatest gift a person can ever receive, the grace of God demonstrated in His Son, Jesus. We all mess up; God calls it sin. We are born that way, but God, in His mercy, sent Jesus to take our punishment for all that sin. When I believed that Jesus came to die for my sin, accepted that gift of grace and asked God for forgiveness,

He became my Heavenly Father.

Thank You, Father, for Your expression of love through Jesus, and thank you Miriam for your expression of love that made a young man better understand God's love. —G. W. Strother

◆

Greater love has no one than this,
than to lay down one's life for his friends.

JOHN 15:13 KJV

◆

Bear ye one another's burdens,
and so fulfill the law of Christ.

GALATIANS 6:2 KJV

◆

For you have been called to live in freedom—
not freedom to satisfy your sinful nature,
but freedom to serve one another in love.

GALATIANS 5:13 NLT

WHAT A FRIEND WE HAVE IN JESUS

What a friend we have in Jesus
All our sins and griefs to bear!
What a privilege to carry
Every thing to God in prayer!

O, what peace we often forfeit!
O, what needless pain we bear!
All because we do not carry
Every thing to God in prayer.

Have we trials and temptations?
Is there trouble anywhere?
We should never be discouraged,
Take it to the Lord in prayer.

Can we find a friend so faithful,
Who will all our sorrows share?
Jesus knows our every weakness—
Take it to the Lord in prayer.

~ HORATIUS BONAR

CONFIDE IN A FRIEND

When you're tired and worn at the close of the day
And things just don't seem to be going your way,
And even your patience has come to an end,
Try taking time out and confide in a friend.

Perhaps he too may have walked the same road
With a much troubled heart and a burdensome load,
To find peace and comfort somewhere near the end,
When he stopped long enough to confide in a friend.

For then are most welcome a few words of cheer,
For someone who willingly lends you an ear.
No troubles exist that time cannot mend,
But to get quick relief, just confide in a friend.

~ AUTHOR UNKNOWN

NO GREATER LOVE

A single, silent tear falls to a sea of LOVE,
A single branch of peace borne on the wings of a dove,
A single man whose LOVE could span the ages,
A single heart of LOVE
that freed others from their cages.
A single crown of thorns placed upon a king,
A single song of sorrow the angels chose to sing.
A single death, a single cross, a single act of LOVE,
A single man a single life, all sent from above.

~ AUTHOR UNKNOWN

◆

*Now we who are strong ought to bear the
weaknesses of those without strength
and not just please ourselves.
Each of us is to please his neighbor
for his good, to his edification.*

ROMANS 15:1, 2 NASB

JESUS' EXTRAVAGANT *Love* IS SUFFICIENT

My grace is sufficient for you.

II CORINTHIANS 12:9 NASB

HIS LAST WORD WAS "JESUS!"

My late husband served the Lord Jesus faithfully from the time he was saved until his death. It was his strong desire to be as much like Jesus as he could possibly be. That meant spending a lot of time studying and meditating on the Word of God, and equally as much time in prayer. It was important for my dear spouse to live a life that was unencumbered by the world. He was the most compassionate and kind person I had ever known. When we married, it was thought that he would not live more than two years and we would not be able to have children, but we were blessed with twelve years together, and three precious children.

It was my husband's great joy to lead our youngest son to the Lord, and all three of our children were baptized in our swimming pool with their dad there to witness that great day in their lives. Daily living became increasingly difficult for my husband: cancer had taken up residence in his body, but he praised the Lord for being all-sufficient in his life. The effects of the illness and the devastating drain on his body and emotions, from the radiation and chemotherapy treatments plagued him, but he continued to trust the Lord to meet his every need. Sick, though he was, he never lost sight of how much the Lord loved him. He talked about all the ways Jesus blessed him and rarely did he complain, even when the blood vessels in his stomach would ooze leaving him doubled over from the pain. He was an inspiration to everyone who knew him. His life was the most pure of anyone I have known throughout my whole life.

As he lay on his death bed, he wanted our children near him. He struggled one last time to hold them close to him. He wanted them to know that it is only Jesus who is able to walk us through the painful times on this earth, and that there would be no more pain or suffering in heaven. Then, with one last frail sound, he called the name that meant everything in life, and now in death, to him...JESUS! He understood the deepest meaning of the all-sufficient Jesus. He left a legacy to our children of a man who never, no matter what came his way, turned away from the One, the only One, who was able to do exceedingly abundantly above all that he could ask, or even imagine. He knew Jesus, and he knew the extravagant love of Jesus. —PMH

Not that we are sufficient of ourselves to think any thing as of ourselves; but our sufficiency is of God.

2 CORINTHIANS 3:5 KJV

Jesus is all the world to me, my life, my joy, my all;

he is my strength from day to day, without him I would fall.

When I am sad, to him I go, no other one can cheer me so;

when I am sad, he makes me glad, he's my friend.

Jesus is all the world to me, my friend in trials sore;

I go to him for blessings, and he gives them o'er and o'er.

He sends the sunshine and the rain,

he sends the harvest's golden grain;

sunshine and rain, harvest of grain, he's my friend.

Jesus is all the world to me, and true to him I'll be;

O how could I this friend deny, when he's so true to me?

Following him I know I'm right, he watches o'er me day and night;

following him by day and night, he's my friend.

Jesus is all the world to me, I want no better friend;

I trust him now, I'll trust him when life's fleeting days shall end.

Beautiful life with such a friend, beautiful life that has no end;

eternal life, eternal joy, he's my friend.

~ WILL L. THOMPSON

◆

With God all things are possible...

MARK 10:27 KJV

I don't care what I see or don't see; what I feel or don't feel;
what I believe or don't believe; what appeals or doesn't appeal;
I'm going to trust Him (with effort and consciously...
'til a habit is renewed) —let Him work everything out.

~ DONALD R. HUMMEL, SR.

＊

For this reason I also suffer these things, but I am
not ashamed; for I know whom I have believed and
I am convinced that He is able to guard what
I have entrusted to Him until that day.

II TIMOTHY 1:12 NASB

＊

Greater is he that is in you, than he that is in the world.

I JOHN 4:4 KJV

＊

Though I walk through the valley of the shadow of death,
I will fear no evil: for thou art with me...

PSALM 23:4 KJV

JESUS, HELP ME!

In every need, let me come to You with humble trust, saying:

Jesus, help me!

In all my doubts, perplexities, and temptations: Jesus, help me!

In hours of loneliness, weariness, and trials: Jesus, help me!

In the failure of my plans and hopes,

in disappointments, troubles, and sorrows:

Jesus, help me!

When others fail me, and Your Grace alone can assist me:

Jesus, help me!

When I throw myself on Your tender love as a Father and a Savior:

Jesus, help me!

When my heart is cast down by failure,

at seeing no good come from my efforts:

Jesus, help me!

When I feel impatient, and my cross irritates me: Jesus, help me!

When I'm ill, and my head and hands cannot work, and I am lonely:

Jesus, help me!

Always, always, in spite of weakness,

falls, and shortcomings of every kind:

Jesus, help me and never forsake me!

~ AUTHOR UNKNOWN

JESUS' EXTRAVAGANT *Love* STRENGTHENS

*But the Lord stood with me
and strengthened me,
so that the message might be
preached fully through me...*

II TIMOTHY 4:17 NKJV

SHARPEN YOUR AXE

A young man approached the foreman of a logging crew and asked for a job. "That depends," replied the foreman. "Let's see you chop down this tree." The young man stepped forward and skillfully chopped down a great tree. Impressed, the foreman exclaimed, "You can start Monday." Monday, Tuesday, Wednesday, Thursday rolled by, and Thursday afternoon the foreman approached the young man and said, "You can pick up your paycheck on the way out today."

Startled, the young man replied, "I thought you paid on Friday."

"Normally we do," said the foreman. "But we're letting you go today because you've fallen behind. Our daily felling charts show that you've dropped from first place on Monday to last place today."

"But I'm a hard worker," the young man objected. "I arrive first, leave last and even have worked through my coffee breaks!"

The foreman, sensing the young man's integrity, thought for a minute and then asked, "Have you been sharpening your axe?"

The young man replied, "No sir, I've been working too hard to take time for that!" —Author Unknown

BENEATH THE CROSS OF JESUS

Beneath the Cross of Jesus, I fain would take my stand,

The shadow of a mighty rock within a weary land;

A home within the wilderness, a rest upon the way,

From the burning of the noontide heat, and the burden of the day.

O safe and happy shelter, O refuge tried and sweet,

O trusting place where Heaven's love and Heaven's justice meet!

As to the holy patriarchs that wonderous dream was giv'n

So seems my Savior's cross to me, a ladder up to Heaven.

There lies beneath it's shadow but on the further side,

The darkness of an awful grave that gapes both deep and wide;

And there between us stands the cross, two arms outstretched to save,

A watchman set to guard the way from that eternal grave.

Upon that cross of Jesus mine eye at times can see

The very dying form of One who suffered there for me;

And from my stricken heart with tears two wonders I confess;

The wonders of redeeming love and my unworthiness.

I take, O cross, thy shadow for my abiding place;

I ask no other sunshine than the sunshine of His face;

Content to let the world go by, to know no gain nor loss;

My sinful self my only shame, my glory all the cross!

~ ELIZABETH CECELIA DOUGLAS CLEPHANE

ALTERED PLANS

I've found that God has altered plans
I made first starting out,
And though it's clear that He knows best...
there have been times of doubt.
The work I do is not the work
I really planned on doing,
And many people in my life
weren't always of my choosing.
I know for sure that it is true...
God has a plan for me,
The paths He's led me down in life
have always been the key...
To lessons learned and growing,
that I would not have done,
The heartaches and the happiness,
the battles fought and won.
Looking back on where I've been,
I've realized just one thing.
Life isn't something that you plan...
it's accepting what it brings.

~ AUTHOR UNKNOWN

For I am convinced that neither death, nor life,
nor angels, nor principalities, nor things present,
nor things to come, nor powers, nor height,
nor depth, nor any other created thing,
will be able to separate us from the love of God,
which is in Christ Jesus our Lord.

ROMANS 8:38, 39 NASB

The Lord is my rock and my fortress and my deliverer;
My God, my strength, in whom I will trust;
My shield and the horn of my salvation,
my stronghold, I will call upon the Lord
who is worthy to be praised;
So shall I be saved from my enemies.

PSALMS 18:2-3 NKJV

He giveth power to the faint; and to them
that have no might he increaseth strength.
Even the youths shall faint and be weary,
and the young men shall utterly fall:
But they that wait upon the LORD
shall renew their strength;
they shall mount up with wings as eagles;
they shall run, and not be weary;
and they shall walk, and not faint.

ISAIAH 40:29-31 KJV

The Lord is my strength and song,
And He has become my salvation.

PSALMS 118:14 NKJV

I KNOW WHO HOLDS TOMORROW

I don't know about tomorrow; I just live from day to day.

I don't borrow from its sunshine for its skies may turn to gray.

I don't worry o'er the future for I know what Jesus said;

And, today, I'll walk beside Him for He knows what is ahead.

Many things about tomorrow, I don't seem to understand.

But, I know Who holds tomorrow, and I know Who holds my hand!

Every step is getting brighter as the golden stairs I climb.

Every burden's getting lighter; every cloud is silver-lined.

There the sun is always shining; there no tear will dim the eye.

At the ending of the rainbow where the mountains touch the sky.

Many things about tomorrow, I don't seem to understand.

But, I know Who holds tomorrow, and I know Who holds my hand!

I don't know about tomorrow; it may bring me poverty.

But, the One who feeds the sparrow is the One who stands by me.

And, the path that is my portion may be through the flame or flood,

But, His presence goes before me and I'm covered with His blood.

Many things about tomorrow, I don't seem to understand.

But, I know Who holds tomorrow, and I know Who holds my hand!

~ IRA F. STANPHILL

JESUS' EXTRAVAGANT *Love* SUSTAINS

Now unto him that is able to keep
you from falling, and to present you
faultless before the presence
of his glory with exceeding joy...

JUDE 1:24 KJV

A HEART IN TURMOIL

In preparation to preach a message, the young ministerial student felt there was no continuity, or good thought development, in his sermon. He questioned why the flock should suffer because of his lack of preparation. A lesson learned came back to mind, almost haunting him: "A fog in the pulpit is a mist in the pew!" His heart seemed empty as he poured over his notes, but he was not attracted to anything. Did he not love? There was certainly no sense of need. Things seemed dull and drab. As he prayed he sensed the real need was that his soul had been corrupted by sin(s). The flesh had drained his soul dry. Confession of his wrong desires and selfish motives brought him some peace. He was finally able to see the Lord work through an unworthy, and unfit vessel. The message finally came together although he did not feel he was as prepared as he needed to be. He continued to pray and when he arrived at the church he found himself moving away to a small out building where he could be alone with the Lord. He cried out for help. "Lord Jesus, I do not feel I am in the place spiritually where my preaching can be received. I need You. Please help me." As he preached that night, he noticed a few actually nodding, which would discourage any seasoned minister, but this young student spoke truth with authority and grace. Afterwards, many came forward to speak with him about the message that Christ had sustained him in his hour of great need. It was the Lord who spoke through him that night and it was the same Lord who gave the increase. From that time on, he recalled the prayer meeting he had that night long ago when he asked the Lord Jesus for help and when he realized the sustaining grace of the One who loved him with His extravagant love...Jesus. —PMH

❖

Heaven and earth shall pass away,
but my words shall not pass away.

MATTHEW 24:35 KJV

❖

It is good for me that I was afflicted,
That I may learn Your statutes.

PSALM 119:71 NASB

❖

Then he stood up and rebuked the wind
and waves, and suddenly all was calm.

MATTHEW 8:26 NLT

SWEET ASSURANCE

Your sweet perfume
Floods through my home
You reveal your Presence
To let me know I'm not alone

Father, so many tears I have cried
As I watched my world fall apart
Yet somehow, You came to me
Filling the void in my broken heart

Yah, My Father, You heard my cry
As I cried to You in desperation
And to my life, You gave
Your glorious restoration

You sent Your Spirit
To comfort my aching soul
Bringing only the kind of peace
That I could ever know

You took the darkness
That turned my day into night
And transformed it
With Your radiant light

You gave me Your Assurance
That no matter what may be
What ever happens
You are here with me.

~ AUTHOR UNKNOWN

For with God nothing shall be impossible.

LUKE 1:37 KJV

◆

Do not be afraid...for I am with you.

JEREMIAH 1:8 NKJV

◆

*For I reckon that the sufferings
of this present time are not worthy
to be compared with the glory
which shall be revealed in us.*

ROMANS 8:18 KJV

◆

*The LORD sustains all who fall and
raises up all who are bowed down.*

PSALM 145:14 NASB

JESUS NEVER FAILS

Earthly friends may prove untrue,
Doubts and fears assail;
One still loves and cares for you,
One Who will not fail.

Though the sky be dark and drear,
Fierce and strong the gale,
Just remember, He is near
And He will not fail.

In life's dark and bitter hour
Love will still prevail;
Trust His everlasting pow'r
Jesus will not fail.

Jesus never fails, Jesus never fails.
Heav'n and earth may pass away,
But Jesus never fails.

JESUS' EXTRAVAGANT *Love* FORGIVES

*But Jesus was saying,
"Father, forgive them; for they
do not know what they are doing."*

LUKE 23:34 NASB

REPENTANCE AND FORGIVENESS
ARE RIVETED TOGETHER

What God hath joined together let no man put asunder. Repentance must go with remission, and you will see that it is so if you think a little upon the matter. It cannot be that pardon of sin should be given to an impenitent sinner; this were to confirm him in his evil ways, and to teach him to think little of evil. If the Lord were to say, "You love sin, and live in it, and you are going on from bad to worse, but, all the same, I forgive you," this were to proclaim a horrible license for iniquity. The foundations of social order would be removed, and moral anarchy would follow. I cannot tell what innumerable mischiefs would certainly occur if you could divide repentance and forgiveness, and pass by the sin while the sinner remained as fond of it as ever. In the very nature of things, if we believe in the holiness of God, it must be so, that if we continue in our sin, and will not repent of it, we cannot be forgiven, but must reap the consequence of our obstinacy. According to the infinite goodness of God, we are promised that if we will forsake our sins, confessing them, and will, by faith, accept the grace which is provided in Christ Jesus, God is faithful and just to forgive us our sins, and to cleanse us from all unrighteousness. But, so long as God lives, there can be no promise of mercy to those who continue in their evil ways, and refuse to acknowledge their wrongdoing. Surely no rebel can expect the King to pardon his treason while he remains in open revolt. No one can be so foolish as to imagine that the Judge of all the earth will put away our sins if we refuse to put them away ourselves.

—C. H. Spurgeon

◆

Him hath God exalted with his right hand to be a Prince and a Saviour, for to give repentance...and forgiveness of sins.

ACTS 5:31 KJV

◆

My grace is sufficient for thee: for my strength is made perfect in weakness. Most gladly therefore will I rather glory in my infirmities, that the power of Christ may rest upon me.

II CORINTHIANS 12:9 KJV

◆

For the word of the cross is folly to those who are perishing, but to us who are being saved it is the power of God.

I CORINTHIANS 1:18 RSV

Do not labor for the food which perishes, but for the food which endures to everlasting life, which the Son of Man will give you, because God the Father has set His seal on Him.

JOHN 6:27 NKJV

✦

THROUGH ME

Through me let there be kind words,
a warm smile, and a caring heart.
Through me let there be a willingness to listen
and a readiness to understand.
Through me let there be dependability,
steadfastness, trust and loyalty.
Through me let there be compassion,
forgiveness, mercy and love.
Through me let there be every quality I find,
O Lord, in Thee.
~ Author Unknown

JESUS! WHAT A FRIEND FOR SINNERS!

Jesus! What a friend for sinners!
Jesus! Lover of my soul;
Friends may fail me, foes assail me,
He, my Savior, makes me whole.
Jesus! What a strength in weakness!
Let me hide myself in Him.
Tempted, tried, and sometimes failing,
He, my strength, my victory wins.
Jesus! What a help in sorrow!
While the billows o'er me roll,
Even when my heart is breaking,
He, my comfort, helps my soul.
Jesus! I do now receive Him,
More than all in Him I find.
He hath granted me forgiveness,
I am His, and He is mine.
Hallelujah! What a Savior!
Hallelujah! What a friend!
Saving, helping, keeping, loving,
He is with me to the end.

~ JOHN WILBUR CHAPMAN

*D*ear Lord, I thank You for this day. I'm blessed because You are a forgiving God and an understanding God. You have done so much for me and You keep on blessing me. Forgive me this day for everything I have done, said or thought that was not pleasing to You. I ask now for Your forgiveness. Please keep me safe from all danger and harm. Help me to start this day with a new attitude and plenty of gratitude. *Amen*

JESUS' EXTRAVAGANT *Love* IS ETERNAL

He that believeth on the Son

hath everlasting life...

JOHN 3:36 KJV

10-4-15

JESUS' LOVE IS EVERLASTING

The Lord Jesus did what no other has ever or will ever be able to do...He came to earth to live as a man, in human form, so He could identify with us. No false god can do that. He did it for you, and for me. Now, that is Love! When we consider the wretchedness of the world He came to from the unspeakable excellence of the heaven He left...now, that is Love! He walked with, and talked with, the weak, the poor, the lame, the evil, the hurting, the bitter...now, that is Love! He reached out with compassion and healed the sick, He made the blind to see, He raised the dead back to life...now that is Love! He brought with Him hope to the wounded and the downtrodden...now, that is love! He suffered the temptations that we fallible human beings experience. For all these things, the nations of the world eagerly seek; but your Father knows that you need these things yet, He bore our sorrows...now, that is love! He endured the agony of the Cross of Calvary, shedding His blood for us, so that we may have life, life eternal...Now, that is LOVE! ~ PMH

✦

SALVATION IS IN JESUS: WHAT HE IS AND
WHAT HE HAS DONE ON THE CROSS IN LOVE!

~ DONALD R. HUMMEL, SR.

O THE DEEP, DEEP LOVE OF JESUS

O the deep, deep love of Jesus, vast, unmeasured, boundless, free!
Rolling as a mighty ocean in its fullness over me!
Underneath me, all around me, is the current of Thy love
Leading onward, leading homeward to Thy glorious rest above!
O the deep, deep love of Jesus,
Spread His praise from shore to shore!
How He loveth, ever loveth, changeth never, nevermore!
How He watches o'er His loved ones,
Died to call them all His own; how for them He intercedeth,
Watcheth o'er them from the throne!
O the deep, deep love of Jesus, love of every love the best!
'Tis an ocean vast of blessing, 'tis a haven sweet of rest!
O the deep, deep love of Jesus, 'tis a heaven of heavens to me;
And it lifts me up to glory, for it lifts me up to Thee!

~ CHARLES WESLEY

◆

Jesus stretched out His hand and touched
him, saying, "I am willing; be cleansed."
And immediately his leprosy was cleansed.

MATTHEW 8:3 NASB

JESUS' TOUCH—
A DEMONSTRATION OF GOD'S LOVE

Neonatal Care Units' staff minister to the needs of premature babies who are not strong enough to go home for weeks, and even months, after their birth. Parents return home to care for other children and to return to work, leaving their babies behind, but visiting as often as is possible. In between parents' visits, their little ones continue to require touch. All the breathing tubes and other medical necessities do not provide the comfort of the touch of a live person. Because hospital staff are aware of this need that promotes healing and growth, a volunteer group has been set up for "Cuddlers." As these dedicated volunteers come in all hours of the day and night to cuddle and stroke babies not much bigger than their own hands, the fragile preemies respond in a positive way. From the moment we enter this life here on earth; we require care, tender care, and touch. Jesus has promised to care for us. He reached out to touch those He ministered to while He lived on earth. His touch continues to be available to us as we grow spiritually. The most tender touch of all is the touch of the Master's hand as He gently places it around one of His children. —PMH

Just as I held and stroked a little Junco until it could fly again.

If, however, you are fulfilling the royal law according to the Scripture, "YOU SHALL LOVE YOUR NEIGHBOR AS YOURSELF," you are doing well. But if you show partiality, you are committing sin and are convicted by the law as transgressors. For whoever keeps the whole law and yet stumbles in one point, he has become guilty of all. For He who said, "DO NOT COMMIT ADULTERY," also said, "DO NOT COMMIT MURDER." Now if you do not commit adultery, but do commit murder, you have become a transgressor of the law. For He who said, "DO NOT COMMIT ADULTERY," also said, "DO NOT COMMIT MURDER." Now if you do not commit adultery, but do commit murder, you have become a transgressor of the law. So speak and so act as those who are to be judged by the law of liberty.

JAMES 2:8-12 NASB

◆

THE LOVE LIFE OF THE LORD JESUS, THINE ALL VICTORIOUS LOVE
SHED IN MY HEART ABROAD; THEN SHALL MY FEET NO LONGER
MOVE, ROOTED AND FIXED IN GOD.

~ CHARLES WESLEY

*J*esus, You love us, no matter what, because You love us from Your heart that is pure. Your love for us includes every part of our being...including the hairs on our heads that You have numbered. Even when we are poor and needy, You think upon us. How great is the sum of Your thoughts toward us. No matter what trials we face here on earth, You, loving Jesus, have ways for us that are higher than the earth. Oh, how thankful we are to You, who loved us first, and who is with us in every circumstance we enter into, and who has promised to be with us surrounding us with Your love and mercy. We can trust You in times of joy, in times of sorrow and trial. How blessed we are to have such Amazing Love! Extravagant, amazing, love. Thank You. *Amen*

With Special Permission

Joe Gallagher Saint Ignatius College Prep '63; Shaefsbury University, Bachelor of Business Administration, Summa Cum Laude 2002; Spouse, Yvonne; Three children; Journalist for four years on local paper; Director of Christian Camp for one week each summer; Secretary and on Board of Director of local church. Resides in TN.

Donald R. Hummel, Sr. (1937-1982) BS, Columbia Bible College, Columbia, SC; ThM, Dallas Theological Seminary, Dallas, TX; Certificates from a number of organizations for outstanding works, both written and public speaking; Ordained minister. Missionary. Was a devoted husband and father. Received numerous awards for excellences in missions and his work with children and the underprivileged. Legacy to his family was years of commitment to seventy journals of exceptional writing about the Christian life.

Patti M. Hummel Widow of the late Rev. Donald R. Hummel, Sr.; Certificate, Moody Bible College, Chicago, IL; Duncan Park Bible College, East Ridge, TN; Pacific & Asia Christian University, Kailua-Kona, HI; UN Christian, Kona, HI; three adult children; author and/or compiler of thirteen books; public speaker; President/Owner, The Benchmark Group, Nashville, TN.

Teresa J. King Spouse, Dave; Two children; Masters, Peabody College of Vanderbilt University, Nashville, TN; Diploma, Emmaus Bible College, Dubuque, IA; Thirty years as Public School Teacher, Nashville, TN; President Middle TN Reading Association; Vice Chairman of Child Evangelism Fellowship of Nashville, TN; Prayer Warrior Coordinator for Horton Haven Christian Camp; Taught a Good News Club in Public School system in South Central TN for four years.

Thomas Lane BA and BD St. Patrick's College Maynooth, Ireland 1989; SSL Pontifical Biblical Institute Rome; STD (doctorate) Pontifical Gregorian University Rome; Ordained into the ministry 1990; Pastor 1994-2004; Assistant Professor, Mount St. Mary's Seminary, Emmitsburg, MD 2004.

Melvin Musgrove Christian Poet; Spouse, Linda; Three children; SS teacher; Prayer and Praise Leader in local church; serves at Christian camp in summers. Resides in TN.

Marcia Russell Born in Detroit; Father's career afforded opportunities to attend many different schools in a number of different states; In her last move with the family, she met her husband John and has been happily married for 15 years.   In addition to being a loving and devoted wife, she is a home school mother to two adopted children.

Linda K. Smith Spouse, Marvin; Three children; Worked several years doing bookkeeping and office work; Course study on lay counseling with The American Association of Biblical Counseling; Public speaker; Mentor hurting/wounded women struggling from abusive childhoods. Community Bible Study Core Leader, Seneca, SC.

G. Wallace Strother b. Tsinan, China to missionary parents; Thirty-three years as Chemist for Dow Chemical; BS Chemistry Louisiana College, Pineville, LA. Masters work at TX A&M; Spouse, Jeanette; four Children; Associate Pastor, First Baptist of Church Hill, TX; Pastored Boles Southern Baptist Church, Boles, AK.

All other works of writers not listed in the biography section are taken from public domain material.

NOTES

NOTES

NOTES

NOTES